MW00583976

Two girls from completely different backgrounds, different times, different countries. One raised in an unhappy, fractured household, never knowing her real father. The other raised by him in a happy, intact family. The story, non linear, ranges from WWII to the present. We cut back and forth from
One searching, the Other having.

Marion, after thirty years of searching on and off has finally found an obituary, Laramie G. Evans, 55 Cherry St. Lyons, NY. He has one son and one daughter. After much deliberation, she writes to the daughter. When Larry Ann opens the letter, a photograph falls to the floor. It's her father, dressed in his WWII uniform. Marion writes, "If this is your father, then I am your sister."

Marion Bornschier (Germany, 1946) worked as a producer and director of documentaries for Swiss and German TV. For many years she concentrated on development issues and made films in Bangladesh, India and South America. Since she retired from TV in 2009, she has built a Renaissance garden in Italy, looked after her grandchildren and – written this book, together with her sister.

Larry Ann Evans (U.S., 1960) lived in Spain for 13 years working on U.S. and International film productions. Her son was born there. She returned to her home town in order to take care of her aged parents and today works there as the Executive Director of the Museum of Wayne County History. She dedicates her free time to the theatre, acting on stage for a community theatre group and directing high school productions.

Marion Bornschier
Larry Ann Evans

SCHWESTER/ SISTER MISSED AND FOUND

Translation of Marion's chapters from German by Andrew Blackwell

First edition 2020
All rights reserved
Copyright © 2020 Marion Bornschier and Larry Ann Evans
Edition 381 | www.edition381.ch

Typefont: Arnhem
Layout: Laila Defelice
Photo Cover: © Marta Lebek | stocksy.com

Print and binding: Books on Demand GmbH, Norderstedt
Paper: Cremeweiss, 90 g/m²

ISBN 978-3-907110-13-3

1 | Marion
Gensungen, Germany – 1946
My Birth

"You did not want to be born," my mother would tell me.

"I had to take endless walks until the contractions finally started."

But was it more that she did not want to let me go? Was she afraid to see me?

When I was able to walk, she told me, I would sometimes run and smash my head straight into the furniture.

"And you, how did you react?"

I asked my mother,

"did you scold me?"

"No," she said, "I understood you, you didn't have an easy life."

Larry Ann
Saratoga, New York – 1967

I Feel Special

I am seven and I have a dress on exactly like my mother's because she had both of our dresses made the same. My mother is Ann Collins, an equine artist who paints for all the rich and famous owners of racehorses. She is somewhere showing the photos of her paintings to a trainer or breeder of a horse, working to get a commission to paint it. My father is with other trainers not far away, but I don't see him. We are on the part of the track where the trainers and breeders hang out with the horses. The horses are resting or eating hay in their stalls, either just raced or waiting to race. Jockeys walk by, dressed in their bright colours for the next race. I am going about my favourite pastime on the track, I am picking up the discarded racing tickets. People on the track sometimes buy 10, 20 different tickets and combinations on 2 or 3 races all at once. After the race is run, they don't remember them all and throw them all down on the ground. That's where I come in. I pick up the ones that I think are the prettiest. Then I take them to my father and he looks them over for me. Once I won $20!

This particular day a man comes up to me and asks me if I know how to call a race, like they do over the loudspeaker when the horses break out of the starting gate and race around the track. Well didn't I just see our horse, Yankee Blaze, win at Pimlico? He even broke the track record.

"Of course I can!"

He didn't lure me off the track into the back of his car as could have happened to a more unfortunate child. He unpacked a portable reel-to-reel tape deck right there in the well trodden dirt and hooked up a microphone which he held in front of me and I called the race. I made up horse's names and inserted some that I knew ...

"Annnnd they're off! The horses are out of the gate and pulling out in front is Belle Donner, followed closely by Gore Vidal and Yankee Blaze is a close third ..."

I could tell he was thrilled. I didn't think that any other kid my age could have even done it.

Afterwards I found my father and told him all about it. Luckily he was able to find this man and they exchanged numbers and we were able to get a copy of the recording made in LP format.

I felt special and this is how I felt very often. I was a fortunate child. My parents loved me and I knew somehow that I had it better than most. Even when my parents were out of work, which later in life I learned was quite often, they never let on. It didn't feel like I had any hardships.

My Mother

My mother is very beautiful. Even as a little girl I can already see that! I am proud of her and love her very, very much. She is quite tall, slender, has beautiful blue-black curls and dark eyes, which can take on a soft, loving expression. But that's rather rare. She often tells me that she was called "the most beautiful girl in Cologne".

Born in 1920, little Ruth grew up in a good middle-class family. She has a quick mind, plenty of temperament and easily wins everyone's heart. But still, she and her younger brother and sister don't have an easy childhood. Their father is often angry and very strict – even with his little darling Ruth. If she does not want to eat, she has to go down into the dark basement with her plate until she's finished eating.

In 1929, when my mother is nine years old, the Great Depression breaks out. My grandfather loses his entire fortune, and from then on he even has to support his mother, who has lost the family's department store and all her savings. Luckily, his mother-in-law in Switzerland has not lost her money, and as my grandfather is a pharmacist, she buys him a pharmacy. Later, a liquor factory is added, and so my grandfather changes from the fun-loving "eternal student" he used to be to a hard-working family man.

My mother is a good student in school, reaching high marks even in mathematics. But in 1939 she drops out of school. Why? Maybe she feels that the world is hers to conquer and why bother with the additional effort of school when admirers swarm around her like moths to a flame. That's what she likes best: to shine. But later in life, she will never forgive herself for dropping out of school.

As the war begins, "all young Germans of both sexes are obliged to serve their people in the Reich Labor Service". My mother's parents want to spare their daughter having to work for the Nazis, so they send her to Davos, Switzerland, where her maternal grandmother, Nana, lives.

Brewster, New York – 1972
My Father

I know three stories about my father, Larry. Two he told me, the third I learned from Uncle Percy. The first is also the only story I have ever heard about my grandfather Albert. My father said he was young, how young I don't know, I always imagined a 10 year old boy, so that would make it 1925. Probably tall for his age, as he said that he gained his full 6'2 height by 14. Lanky, thin, and hot because it was summer in Brooklyn and he told me he had been playing in the street. Probably stick-ball or baseball. He came running in the house to get a glass of water and stopped short. His father was there and had just finished waxing or polishing the floor. My father said he was very thirsty after playing, but between him and the kitchen was a long hall that had just been polished and his father at the end of it, at the entrance to the kitchen.

"I was thirsty and came in for a drink of water ..."
  (Pause)
  "Well, come and get a drink then ..."
  (Pause)
  "You just finished polishing the floor ..."
  "Yes. But come on anyway ..."
  My father hesitates.
  "No, I'll come back later ..."
  "No, come on. Get a glass of water."
My father gingerly steps foot onto the freshly polished floor, making his way toward his father and the kitchen and the water. Step by step closing the gap. When he reaches his father and is about to pass him and enter into the kitchen, his father backhands his son with such force that the boy goes flying down the hall and smashes up against the back door.

"That will teach you not to walk on a freshly polished floor."

The second story is very short. My father had two sisters and a brother. Percy, the brother, was the oldest, then came Larry, then Millie, then the youngest, another girl, Cecile. In one of the houses where my father lived with his family in Brooklyn he said that the door frames were quite high and he used to take his sister Cecile and hang her there. He would leave her, clutching at the door frame with her fingers. He thought it was quite funny. I imagine he took her down after awhile. I don't want to give the impression that he was cruel. He never hung me from the door frame.

The third story was from Uncle Percy and he told it to me after my father had died. "We were boys," Uncle Percy starts, "and we were making our way through a park after school and another boy was taunting us. He wouldn't stop and instead of your father telling him to stop he took this boy and started beating the crap out of him. He stopped when the kid was a bloody mess. There was such rage and anger in your dad at that time. I think he would have killed the kid if I hadn't stopped him."

That didn't seem like my father. He never beat the crap out of me and he got plenty mad at me. One good smack on the behind with his great big hand is what I got. Who is this boy who beats others to a bloody mess? Why was he so angry? Did it come from his own father's cruelty? Or because he was so poor? And why are these stories so important to me? I guess I'm trying to figure out the man who was my father. He   my mother when he was 44. He had whole other lives that he lived before then and he let none of them be known. He was in WWII but he hardly ever talked about it.

3 | Marion
Cologne, Germany – 1941
Mother's First Marriage

When the war breaks out, my mother returns to Germany to her parents' house. Disheartened by her first love which started and ended in Davos, she enrolls in a photography school in Weimar – which, according to West Germans, is the most boring place on Earth. It does not take her long to catch the eye of a very rich bon vivant who brings her back to Cologne. E. is a lawyer and comes from a family whose wealth was made in the medical profession. My mother admires the ingenuity and worldly appearance of this man who is fifteen years her senior. But one might have thought she would notice his weak character too. When my grandmother proudly announces her daughter's engagement to him during a ladies' tea, a woman at the table exclaims "Nonsense. My daughter is the fiancée of Dr. E.! " But E. keeps the promise of matrimony made to my mother and the two marry in November, 1941.

Germany, thrilled by its military success, in a short time has overrun Poland, Denmark, Norway, Belgium, the Netherlands, Luxembourg and even France. The "arch-enemy" is defeated. At this time, the Russian campaign too is being waged.

Even though it is the middle of the war, Ruth's father throws a fairytale wedding for his daughter. The lavish menu includes:
- Goose liver pate, toast with butter, served with port wine
- Oxtail soup
- Fish dish with mushrooms
- Roe deer leg in cream sauce
- Glazed apples with cranberries
- Red cabbage, duchess potatoes
- Peach Melba with pastry

- Moselle and Rhine wines, red and white
- Mocha, liquors, cognac

For E. my mother is a gem. Every dress becomes her, every piece of furniture she decorates the house with looks like it has always belonged there. E. overwhelms his young wife with clothes, jewellery and fur. The wedding photograph shows a happy, laughing couple. In the second row are my mother's parents. But next to E. is his mother, clinging to his arm. There is no doubt that this woman will never get over having to hand over her idolised only son to another woman. So, as a tribute, E. must distribute the wealth and presents equally between his mother and his wife. Always the same amount of attention, jewels and furs to each of them.

It doesn't take long until it becomes clear to my mother that E. has a drinking problem. By night he starts acting as if he were a bachelor again, spending his time in drunken orgies with prostitutes, black marketeers and other sordid types that use the war to make money, as he does. By day, he keeps his nose clean, working as a lawyer. This allows E. and my mother to lead a life of luxury but she is horrified and disgusted by the man whose name I bear until the day I marry.

On the night of June 30, 1943, the war hits home. Five hundred British bombers leave Cologne in ruins. My mother survives the disaster in an air-raid shelter. She and all the other family members are left uninjured, but her house and that of her parents are completely destroyed. She moves with E. to an upscale hotel next to a cathedral, both of which remain intact, and life just keeps going on throughout the bombings. But something has changed: my mother begins suffering from terrible anxiety. It is decided that she moves to her aunt and cousin's house in Bavaria for a while. The south of Germany has so far been spared the bombings. E. stays in Cologne.

My mother's cousin, Inge, is one year older than her. She is a pretty young woman, slim like a boy, and works as a press photographer. She is documenting the war and even continues to do so after the war, during the reconstruction.

War Torn Germany,
city of Cologne.
My home town, 1945

I remember my Aunt Inge, whom we visited frequently during my entire childhood. She filled big albums with her photographs of me. I also kept in close contact with her as an adult, because she was my role model. We spent hours looking over her photographs, of which every one had its own story. I liked one in particular: it was just of a crowd of people. Inge took this picture during the currency reform in 1948, when every German citizen received 40 new German Marks. In order to get the best shot of the endless queues of people, she climbed onto a tall scaffold. Her male colleagues laughed at her, they were sure that the girl could neither climb, nor get a good shot. But she did both and left the men gaping in complete surprise.

Inge is the only person I know that I can ask about the American officer, back in the war. But each time I broach the subject, Inge declines, saying she does not remember, it was so long ago.

"But you must remember something!" I insist.

All I get out of her is that he was a tall, dark-haired man with a long, slender face.

Larry Changes his Name

My father's name is Laramie, but not really, it's George. I found out that his middle name was George when I was five or six years old. We were living in Florida, my friend Todd and I somehow, as only small children can, got ahold of my father's wallet and saw his driver's license. It said "Laramie George Evans." "George! Like the first president!" we said and proceeded to come up with a military salute for him as he came in the house. We stood at attention, on the small concrete step in the warm yellow sunlight and said, "Good afternoon, President George Washington." He laughed, so far above us with his 6'2 stature and said, "Why thank you. Carry on men."

Many years later, he told me a story about how his name changed from George to Laramie. He said he was too young to sign up for the army during World War II, so he went in under his older brother Percy's name who wanted to continue in school. Once in the army and after quite a few jokes and ribbing due to the name, Percy, he came clean to his superiors and started the process of getting his name changed back to George. He sent away the proper paperwork to start the name change. It came back "Percy Evans," so he tried again. I guess the paperwork was sent to Laramie, Indiana, because when it came back this time, it read, "Laramie George Evans."

I always believed my dad, why shouldn't I? And I was pretty bad at math, because if I had thought about it, the Americans entered WWII in 1942, my father would have been twenty-seven in 1942. He would have been old enough, he would not have had to enter under his brother's name.

Years later after my father died, my uncle Perry, Percy, told another version of that story.

"It was in 1933. We were a very, very poor family living in Brooklyn. We had no food, we were all basically starving. It was during the Depression and our father couldn't hold a job. Our parents had sent us boys to our aunt's house so she could take care of us. I think this affected Larry more than any one of us for some reason. I think all of his anger was born out of

CCC workers with picks and shovels building road in Utah.

the poor immigrants life that we lived. In comes President Roosevelt with his fireside chats and the New Deal was born. One of the programs of the New Deal in 1933 was the Civilian Conservation Corps, the CCC, which put thousands of young men to work on projects in national forests, parks, and public lands."

I found out that in order to sign up for the CCC, a person had to be eighteen. In 1933 my father was seventeen about to turn eighteen. So he went in under his brother Percy's name and same story, just a different year. Not fighting in the war like what would happen 10 years later, but fighting poverty, fighting heritage, fighting family. He signed in under his brother's name, letting Percy continue in school. Funny, Uncle Percy always said that Larry was the smarter one, "He never had to study – just look at it and he knew it."

So, my father was sent to Montana to create, work the land, plant trees, build a national park. When he came back home, he was no longer George Irving Evans, he was Laramie George Evans. The first step to reinventing himself.

An Unexpected Guest

I'm four or five years old and like to leaf through my mother's
many photo albums. They are nicely designed. Apart from the
photos, there are colourful cutouts from magazines and mat-
ching clippings from advertisements. Among the volumes
there is one that interests me in particular. The one where she
has put pictures of her admirers. I always skim these pages –

until I arrive at the photos of
a man in uniform with thick,
black eyebrows.

"Who is this man, mom-
my?" I want to know again
and again.

She has stuck a Lucky
Strike advertisement next to
the photos and a cartoon
showing a soldier leaning
against a jeep. There is something on the Jeep in a language that remains incom-
prehensible to me long after
I learn to read: "Une nuit
d'amour ..."

April 30, 1945, the day Hitler
commits suicide: most of
the Bavarian towns are in

Mother's picture
gallery of the officer
in uniform

ruins. The American troops capture Munich without encountering significant opposition. On the 1st of May they reach the southern suburbs. Everything that has legs runs onto the streets. Some to see the victorious enemy with their own eyes, the others – to which my mother, her aunt Amsel and her cousin Inge belong – to greet the liberators. The three women, one prettier and brisker than the other – even Inge's mother who is in her mid-forties can still keep up – attract a good-looking officer. He chats a little with the ladies, who muster all their English skills, gives them cigarettes and asks them where they live. The three provide the information. But when they go home, they get scared. Did they behave too naïvely? What will happen to them? However, the evening passes quietly and without any events. It is only the next morning that the surprise comes: on the garden fence, a large cross has been drawn with chalk. A sign that this house is protected. Reports of mass soldiering and looting in private homes are now making the rounds in the village. Later, most homeowners even have to vacate their homes to Americans. But my mother, her aunt, and her cousin are completely spared. What's more: they even get a lodger.

Three War Stories from Larry

My father was in WWII but he only ever told me a very few stories about the war. Well like I said he was a man of very few words, but he did like to tell a good story. The first story takes place when he was in France and got separated from his platoon. He said he came upon a French farm and the couple that lived there gave him shelter for the night, possibly for a couple of days, maybe even hiding him from the Germans. Before he left they gave him a bottle of wine, in thanks to all the Americans who had come over to fight in this war in Europe. He then said he was able to get behind enemy lines and help rescue a few of his platoon that had been captured. When I heard this story I would try to imagine my father in his combat uniform, carrying a gun, ducking under barbed wire in the dead of night, sneaking between tanks and and Germans in long coats smoking cigarettes to liberate some of his friends.

The next story is pretty horrific, I don't really know where it took place but I did find out that his platoon was near Buchenwald concentration camp when it was liberated. Members of his Battalion were allowed to go and tour it, if you can imagine. Men interested in going were brought to this place where torture, starvation, gas chambers and human ovens were used to exterminate the Jews. The men were shown the torture chambers, the crematorium where charred remains of human bodies were still inside several of the ovens, the laboratory where experiments were carried out, then onto the rest of the grounds. Near the Buchenwald garden and down the hall was a massive grave where over 5000 prisoners were buried. My father didn't give me any of this information, all he said is that he and his platoon were making their way through Germany, the Allies were winning, the Germans were being defeated and as they made their way across a field, he realized the ground was moving under his feet. Moving, he said, writhing he said, because they were walking on top of a massive grave where bodies were thrown on top of bodies, some dead, some still living, and then they were all covered up with earth.

Lastly, he told me that even though he had served his time in the war, when some of the troops were being sent home, Patton requested that his platoon be held over after the war for occupational duties. The first week of June the battalion carried out these duties in Eggenfelden, about 70 miles from Munich. Here the battalion was to maintain law and order among the civilians and capture any German soldiers trying to evade the American authorities. I seem to remember that he once told me he was judge for a day. Erroneously I thought that was at the famous Nuremberg Trials. Now it looks like if he were judge for a day, it would have been here, in Eggenfelden.

Those were the only stories I know from the entire time he was in the war. From 1942 to1945 he told me only these few things, but oh, there was so much more to tell ...

Researching his platoon, the 456th AAA (AW) Battalion, I found a book written by John F. Hendrickson online. It's only location was in the library at the University of Pittsburgh. The local library in Lyons was able to get me a copy to read and when I saw the book, I realized I had seen a copy in my house! I looked in the small library of old books in the dark little den, and finally found the book. It was a little warped as books are when they sit on a shelf without being touched for many years. Under his biography it said that he was Battalion Sgt. Major and decorated with three medals: Good Conduct, Sharpshooter, and Bronze Star. Sharpshooter? That seemed so strange to me. When I was about 12 my mother wanted to teach me how to shoot, he was opposed to it and I was disappointed that he wouldn't let this woman who had grown up in the wild west teach me something that she was obviously good at. Turns out he was the dead shot.

The book went on to say he was also the Battalion's top-ranking noncommissioned officer, a Personnel Officer for an anti-aircraft artillery battalion in Germany enlisted in the service from Oct. 1, 1942 to July 13, 1945. My father never said why he entered the army, but his records say he was an Assistant Engineering Aide for the United States Army Engineers in Miami Beach. Maybe it was just a logical step for him to enter into the army, as he was already working for the military.

Serving in WWII was probably life changing, not only because he served for three years but also because he made something of himself in the army. There were probably many more stories he could have told me.

Marion
Munich, Germany – 1945
A Love Story?

I would love to believe in a romantic love story about my mother and the American officer. I wish it was a love story, because the fantasy of being a child of love is beautiful and comforting. But when I think about the time they spent under the same roof, I really can't imagine what it was like. Mother, how did you talk to each other? Was it in French? Did the GI live weeks or just days in the house with you, Inge and your aunt? Did either of them know about or notice the affair? Probably not. But I'll never know because I never asked her. One thing I can well imagine: it must have caused a tingling sensation to do something so forbidden.

My mother was a married woman – and her lover a married man.

These soldiers, far from home and from their girlfriends or wives – some of course enjoyed flirting with the German girls or had affairs. That was forbidden though, and not just for personal moral reasons. After the invasion of the Allied troops, General Eisenhower had proclaimed "We come as a victorious power, not as oppressors." But it didn't mean the soldiers were allowed to fraternise with the defeated enemy. And the German women? Who would have been adverse to a flirt with the heroes? But it was completely shameful to really get involved with a GI. The "Ami-Liebchen", who allegedly threw themselves at the Americans in exchange for items such as chewing gum and cigarettes, became a public ridicule. My mother was certainly very afraid of being seen as one.

But some did find lasting love. After the end of the war, 20,000 "soldier brides" emigrated to the United States to marry their lover.

During my childhood years, my mother and I visit Aunt Amsel and cousin Inge regularly, and they often talk about the year they spent together in Munich during the war. But the romance

with the American officer is always left out. I learned of it when I was fourteen, years later. The three women enjoyed their household without men. They did not suffer any shortage, while food and clothing were forcibly rationed for the majority of the German population.

Charmed by the winners, German women let themselves be courted

My mother, her aunt and Inge always had food, a bottle of wine, sometimes even cigarettes. These were treasures that E. brought. He continued to work in Cologne, had good friends in the black market and regularly came to visit his wife, crossing the war zone in a wood carburettor car.

Since I know about the history of the Second World War from high school, these stories sound almost obscene to me. How could you have fun in 1944 without having a bad conscience? Knowing that millions of people died at the front, in the gas chambers, burned alive in the bombings, starved to death, or shot fleeing? As a child the following song was sung to me by my nanny and it always made me cry:

"Fly away may beetle,
father is at war,
your mother is in Pomerania,
But Pomerania has burned down,
Fly away may beetle."

My mother does not experience any real hardships during the war. And yet, the fate of the Jews must have touched her and also been a topic between her and her lover. The emancipated, exhausted survivors of concentration camps were seen everywhere at the end of the war, expelled from the camps by the SS in order to erase the traces of horror. It really must hit the American hard that he was a Jew himself. Why else would he have revealed this to my mother?

I'm Jewish

"English!? You're not English. You're Jewish!"

What? It was as if a bomb had dropped.

My cousin Amee and I are vacationing with our husbands and children in the Catskills and now I'm just staring at her, wondering if she is speaking a foreign language to me ... What is she talking about?

"I'm not Jewish. My father was born in England and he said some of his family came from Alsace Lorraine and my mother's family is Irish and German."

Amee just looked at me and said, "Your father may have been born in England, but our entire family, all the Evans and the Newmans, are Jewish."

"What?"

Daddy said I was English. Jewish? Not that I thought it was bad to be Jewish, later I would think it was pretty cool, but at the time, I couldn't wrap my mind around why no one told me. Did mommy know? Too late to ask because they are both dead.

"Are you sure?" I ask my cousin.

"Of course I'm sure. I think the name was actually Evansky and changed to Evans when they got to the states."

Some time after this while talking to my Uncle Percy, he said that although the family was Jewish, they weren't practicing Jews. He remembered having a bar mitzvah, but just two years later, his younger brother Larry was never given one.

After that vacation I looked on the Internet to see if I could find out more information about my new found heritage and ended up emailing a Rabbi. Well he informed me that really,

I wasn't Jewish since only my father was Jewish and the heritage is traced down the matriarchal lines.

I guess in California where Amee and her husband live, the Rabbis are more liberal minded. In any case, why was that hidden from me? What other secrets are out there?

An Affair with Consequences

When did the American officer return home? When the war was finished, the American government sent more than two million GIs home in just two months.

Anyway, he must have been gone when my mother realises she's pregnant. The world must have come crashing down on her. Is the child E.'s? She's been married to him for four years and not gotten pregnant. Is the child the GI's? In terms of

time, either man could be the father. Ruth is in turmoil. She has no idea what to do. She accuses her mother of not informing her about contraception. Her mother on the other hand keeps wondering why Ruth is so against having this child. My mother even writes to her mother-in-law telling her that she wants to break up with her husband. Her mother-in-law writes back:

"Dear Ruth, you knew about E.'s faults and the kind of company he keeps before you married him. And, hell, are you sure this is the right moment for a divorce, now that a baby is on the way?"

Navy aircraft carrier
in operation
"Magic Carpet"

Later, my mother will tell me that she actually tried to abort me.

"But once you were born, I was happy," she assures me. I hear what she's saying, but I'm not sure she's really being truthful and I'm hurt and mad at her.

But back then Ruth keeps the affair secret. She wants to call the baby Miryam, if it is a girl. E. finds the name "too Jewish". What irony of fate!

As soon as I'm born, E. has a fit. He doesn't believe that this little thing, with the olive skin, the black button eyes and a nose which, he says, looks more like a socket than a nose, is his child. Was he suspicious of, or did he even meet the American who was staying with the three women? I don't know, and I have no idea how he and my mother solved this crisis. For sure, E. loved my mother, and he could be generous. Maybe he thought these doubts of his would go away. In any case, he buys a villa for the family in Godesberg near Bonn. We live on the upper floor and E.'s mother moves in on the lower floor.

6 | Larry Ann
| Los Angeles, California – 1981
| **A Little Boy**

I picked up the phone and dialed information. I was alone in my Hollywood bungalow that day. The house was located behind another house, off of Buena Vista Blvd. None of the noise of Sunset Blvd trickled down so it was very quiet. The living room was cool in the shade of a large tree in the front yard. Dust filtered through the air as I waited for information to answer. How many B. Evans could be located in Chicago?

I had been living in Los Angeles for a couple of years now, moved up here with my best friend M. But I had just recently rented this house with my friend, R., who then turned into my boyfriend. We could say first real boyfriend, since I was a virgin ,till twenty-one.

I'm on the phone dialing information because I had recently visited my parents in Lyons. I remember I was sitting with my father and he was opening his wallet. Going through the pictures. It seems that we were talking about his favorite picture of me. He had many pictures of me in his wallet. His little girl. One of the two of us – me three years old on my pony, he standing next to us. Another of me in diapers, bending over to smell a rose. Me looking like a 1930's movie star leaning out of the car with a seal skin coat on. Then come the pictures of me that I had taken by my friend K. in Los Angeles. These were studio-like shots, very artsy – costumes, bold looks. Then I flipped over some of the photos and there in the back of the wallet was a picture of a little boy ... A little boy that looked very much like me. But how could this be. I was an only child. I had no male cousins, maybe a cousin of a cousin?

"Who is this, Daddy?"

No answer. My mother walks into the room.

"Who's this little boy that looks like me?"

"You might as well tell her, Larry."

Tell her what, I think ...

"Information. City and State?"

"Chicago, Illinois. B. Evans"

My father remained silent. But that really is nothing new. Again, he was a man of few words, making those that he did say more important. My mother answered.

"Your father was married before."

I was 21 and an only child and I tried really hard to wrap my mind around this new tidbit of information: my father was married before and this then was his little boy. The boy was smiling in the picture, he was six, maybe eight. It was like a portrait or school picture.

"What's his name?"

"B." Seems like my father had found his voice. "B.K. Evans."

Why don't I know this boy? Is he dead, I thought.

"Do you talk to him? Do you see him?"

"You father sends him money."

"When's the last time you saw him?" I ask, pretty stunned now.

"Well, Larry Ann, I last saw him when he was 7."

I guess my stunned expression needed more than that.

"My first wife had already found someone else and in those days you didn't have two fathers, one stepped out of the picture. The last time I saw him, I gave him a camera and that was it."

"Your first wife? Mommy is your second?"

Again that tricky silence ...

"No, but I'm the last," my mother announced, winking.

"There are three B. Evans in the directory. Do you want them all?"

"Yes, please."

I called the first one. No answer. I dialed the second one, there was an answer machine on. I didn't think the whole, "Hi! I'm your sister" would be too good on a message so I hung up. I called the third number ... It rang ...

A man answered.

"Hello?"

"B.Evans?"

"Yes."

"B.K. Evans?"

"Yes."

I'm getting more nervous and excited at every yes.

"Is your mother's name ...?"

"Yes ..."

"Well if your grandfather is a lawyer and his name is ... Then I'm your sister!"

The conversation with B. was nice, but short. No great revelation was found and we actually didn't talk again for many years. I hung up the phone still feeling like an only child.

Bad Godesberg, Germany – 1946

Milk and Honey

It's 1946/47 and Germany is starving. Masses of desperate people from the towns take trips to the countryside in overcrowded trains, in order to exchange their remaining valuables for flour, eggs and bacon from the farmers. Infants and toddlers die because there is no milk. How unfair life can sometimes be! I spend my first two years in a nice big house with a garden. We are privileged to have a gardener and a nanny. The gardener, Mr. White and my nanny, "Aunty" Christel love me. Mr. White is proud to always be able to provide me with the freshest vegetables.

Of course you can not buy everything that a spoiled city dweller wants with money, but Nana is in Switzerland where there was no war. I'm barely a year old on our first visit to see her. After a fourteen-hour trip, my mother, grandmother and I reach the Swiss border in one of the few trains that travel long distances. Again we have to wait. I pass the long hours by holding on to the mesh of the border fence and try to pull myself up to a standing position. By the time the waiting is over, I have actually learned to walk! On the other side, Nana is waiting. How relieved she is that her family has survived the war and how happy to hold her first great-granddaughter in her arms! A shopping fever takes a hold of my mother and grandmother. Nana has to go to the bank three times to withdraw more money so that the ladies can buy clothes, powdered milk and other food. The day is coming to an end and we have to leave. Since we are restricted in terms of how much we can bring back into Germany, we pile on the clothes, one on top of the other, so we end up looking roly-poly when we cross the border. The customs officer looks at us and smiles: "You have been eating well over there I see ..."

One day, out of the clear blue sky, a letter arrives from the USA., probably forwarded to my mother by Inge.

March 22, 1948
My dearest Ruth:
Dearest Dearest Ruth, it seems like a 1000 years since I last saw you. It has been a long time almost two and a half years since I last held you in my arms and said Adios, until we meet again. I wonder if you ever left Germany and went to Switzerland. I wonder if you have been thinking of me as I have thought of you. Many many things have happened since my return to the United States and many times I have been almost driven to desperation just thinking of you. Tell me (liebschen) do you still feel the same or has the passage of time made you forget me.

Letter from
March 22, 1948

36

I haven't written until now because I had to go through almost a living hell before I found out that my marriage would never work out. It is a long story and a very complicated one and I will tell you all about it in my next letter. This letter is sent in the hope that it will reach you somehow. When you receive it please answer immediately and tell me all about yourself. Tell me everything that has happened since I left, but most of all tell me honestly, tell me truly, Do you still love me. I must know Darling I must know if you still feel the same way about me because I have never stopped loving you. I imagine I always will. I am trying to get matters straightened out here in the next few months so that I can be free again, then I am going to Switzerland to see you. So please my dear one write soon and tell me that you haven't forgotten our vows to each other. If you can't put the proper words in English then write me in French or German. This is all for now my dear, write me soon, I am eagerly awaiting your letter.

   With all my love,

   Larry Evans

A second letter arrived, dated two months later. My mother probably thought she hid her secret correspondence well from her husband, but it wouldn't be long before he found them.

May 10, 1948

Dearest darling Ruth!

Today I received your letter and, to say the least, I was overwhelmed. Why didn't you write to me and let me know that we have a daughter. When you sent me the photographs, why didn't you send a message telling me what happened. Nearly two and a half years have passed since we said "au revoir". Remember that we did not say farewell because I knew that one day I would come back to you? Marion is a little darling, and I certainly see a lot of you when I look at her pictures. Certainly I love her because she's a part of me, and in a way I'm happy it happened because I believe that it made your love for me even stronger while I was gone. What will your aunt think of me and also Inge. I can imagine that they were shocked. Dear, how is the baby's birth certificate issued? Does it have my name? I wish that the girl be known as Marion Evans and anyone who wants a confirmation that she is my daughter can write to me and I will confirm it for the files.

Dearest Ruth, maybe I'm crazy, at least many people tell me, but for some reason I had the feeling that you had a child. Something always told me that maybe there was one. I do not know how to explain it, I liked the feeling.

Do you have a big picture of me so Marion recognizes me when she sees me?

I could start telling you what has happened since I came home. I have spent the most miserable years of my life. The only consolation I got from my marriage was a sweet little boy, my son Barry who is 16 months old now, and that's the only thing I'm sorry to lose now that my wife and I want to separate. We plan to divorce as soon as I can afford it. (...)

Love to you and Marion
yours always,
Larry

Would You Like a Sister?

I remember the day. Even more clear than yesterday. I was nine. I went into my parents' bedroom. They were both sitting in bed, sitting up. Happy. The sunlight shines onto the north wall, illuminating it a soft and bright white. The floor is warm on my bare feet and the off white furniture is pretty with its gold trim.

"Larry Ann ..." my father says.

"Hmm?" I'm still a bit sleepy, not fully awake.

"Would you like a little brother or sister?"

Now I'm wide awake. The sun filled room has lost my attention. I look at my father relaxed in bed. Long legs under the covers, one knee up. Thick dark hair never disheveled. Thick eyebrows raised.

I look at my mother. Long legs under the covers. Both legs straight, with toes pointed even though I can't see them. Ash blonde hair with soft curls in place. Small smile playing about her lips. I looked back at them, possibly after a quick study of my toes. They looked so calm and happy I seemed to not want to break the mood, but a smaller brother or sister? What about my toys? They would have to be shared. My parents' attention? I'm sure that abstract idea hadn't formed in precisely those words, but the thought, the feeling was somehow there.

"No, I don't want a little sister or brother," I said, and jumped on the bed with them. "I want a big sister or brother!"

There was a subtle change in my father's expression and a small laugh from my mother. That is all I remember of that day or that year or that time. But I remember that as clear as if it were yesterday ...

A Turning Point

Is there a woman who would not be touched by Larry's words! Three years after the "Au revoir" my mother starts to exchange love letters with him.

Does she think it over a long time before she answers? I do not have her letter, but there are two months between Larry's two letters. He is overjoyed with the baby. Is it a moment of happiness for my mother? Has she seen a turning point in her life, a way out of her marriage with a husband she doesn't love and who doubts that he is the father of her child? Marrying Larry would be a chance to live without a lie.

But can he offer her the future she dreams of? Love, yes, certainly, but luxury? Safety? Should she make a new start in a completely unknown world? Can she do it? I have no idea if it cost her sleepless nights to make a decision. Because Larry has also written that he must establish a new existence after his return from the war and after quitting the army. He was forced to go into debt in order to pay for his divorce and to start a business. The so-called War Brides Act allowed American soldiers to bring a bride from overseas to the US. Five thousand dollars had to be deposited in a blocked account. Under this condition, the US government paid for the passage and granted a three-month visitor's visa. They had to get married before the three months were over.

"Who will wait three months, we'll do it right away, won't we, dear," Larry writes.

But my mother holds on to her marriage. I do not know how she tells Larry, or even whether she writes to him again at all after his second letter. All I have is a third letter from him saying he was very worried because he had not heard from her in five weeks.

I imagine my mother being very nervous during this time. Luckily, there is alsoAunt Christel. As I said, I love her very much. She is the same age as my grandmother. Small like a child, with rickety curved legs that testify early malnutrition. She is the most patient nanny you can imagine. She wears her sparse hair tightly tied in a knot. I don't know how many times a day I pull the hair pins out of that nodule with a squeak of joy. And every time she just puts it back together. When she gives me a bath, I'll play with the water and spill it until we're both wet. She sleeps in a room in the attic, and when she goes upstairs, I want to follow her. I manipulate the latch of my playpen until it opens. And then I crawl up the steep wooden stairs in order to find my nanny. Each time when I appear upstairs, Aunt Christel gets the shock of her life – I could have fallen down the stairs! My mother, however, gets angry with me. She is jealous of Aunt Christel and makes fun of her crooked legs. And because she is the one who washes my diapers, they all call her "Aunt Pee". Only much later, during my psychoanalysis, do I feel the pain of being torn between two people that you love.

One day, a young woman turns up at the house with her little boy. E.'s mother knows her from before the war, my mother is told. She says her house has burned down and she and her son, who is only a few months younger than me, have no place to live. It is decided that she can live downstairs with old Mrs. E. and run her household. Aunt Christel, my nanny, finds little Michael a little stupid, he does not even respond to his name. No wonder – his name isn't reallyMichael, but E. – like his father. What a terrible truth! My mother finds out because there is an argument between E. and the woman which echoes

41

through the entire house. The woman is jealous because I, the child on the upper floor, have everything – a stroller, clothes, baby food, things that Nana regularly sends from Switzerland to Germany – and her son, nothing.

The disaster happens some time later. My mother is having a terrible argument with her husband. Does it wake me up? Do I get up from my bed and see her leaving? Or do I only realise the next morning that she is gone? Even later, Aunt Christel never tells me anything about it. She is as silent as a grave about everything unpleasant – like about the nuns in the Catholic orphanage where she grew up. When I ask her about my mother leaving the house, she just raises her eyebrows and makes a gesture that I know from her and which means, "Let's talk about something else, dear child." She wouldn't tell me how long my mother left me in Godesberg with her and E. I doubt that E. did anything to comfort me in this situation, where nobody knew what would happen. I doubt it because he never treated me like a daughter. I cannot remember ever sitting on his lap.

Larry Ann
Motels, Houses and Barns – 1965–1970
My Daddy and Me

We were a family that didn't go camping and we didn't take vacations. It always seemed to me that our whole life was made up of vacations, we packed a lot. Maybe that's because for part of every year we lived in motels. In Saratoga we stayed in a motel where the owners had 12 children! That was the best. Six of them could go in the pool in the morning and the other six in the afternoon. I loved going to that motel and couldn't wait until after the Saratoga Sales, the third week in August, came around and I would go from Nana's to that motel to meet my parents. When we went to Belmont Race track in New Jersey, sometimes we stayed in a motel there. The pools were my back yards and the parking lot my street. My father taught me how to ride a bicycle in the parking lot of a motel and my mother taught me to swim in the motel pools. It was always a treat when daddy was there with us and not at the track working. He would dive into the pool like an Olympic swimmer. His feet always together, his arms, legs and long body straight as an arrow. My mother taught me to swim, but my father taught me to dive. "Dive right in, Larry Ann."

We have been moving since I was born, we not only lived in motels, we also lived in houses and a barn once. The barn with dark redwood walls and the Native American rugs on the floors that always travelled where we did. I remember living in a white house with a coconut tree in the backyard in Florida, rolling hill horse farms in NY and Maryland, and I went to more schools than anybody I kew. I was pretty good at making new friends wherever we went, but it was never easy. One time we lived in the state of Washington. The horse farm was in Tenino, and the woods next to the farm contained these immense trees. Pristine forests, cold, soil filled streams. We lived there exactly long enough for me to think it would be our forever home, one year. I was in the 2nd grade and my mother and I with a few other kids from the farm would take long walks. This was the first time in my life that I had time with her because she wasn't painting.

One day, daddy came home and said "Pack," to mommy. She looked at me, that beautiful blonde hair just jiggling, "Pack." A few protests further and off I was in my room packing. I learned a little while later that we packed up and left because Daddy, who had lived most of his best years in Florida, couldn't stand that it rained 250 days out of the year. But to me it seemed we left a little paradise. Now that I think about it, it must have been hard for my mother to not be near the east coast race tracks and prospective commissions of her equine art.

What he said, was what we did, whether it was "Pack," or "Dive right in." He was stern and strict, fair and kind. When I was small and going to some school and living in some motel, if he took me to school then we would stop off and get eggs and sausage at the diner together. These were moments I cherished. If we missed the ice cream man, he would say, "Larry Ann, get in the car. We're going to find him." To this day my favorite sausage are the links we ate together and my favorite ice cream the Italian ice that came with a wooden flat spoon.

There is a picture that shows exactly how I felt about being with my father when I was young. In the picture I must be about five. I remember that Mommy and Daddy were at the bar and I was sitting in the middle. I was the only child ever allowed in the bars with my parents and that too made me feel special. I always was given a Shirley Temple or a Ginger Ale on the rocks. In the picture I'm drinking a Ginger Ale. I'm sitting on the left and my father is on the right. He has a big smile on his face, smiling at the camera. He is a bit in the background. I am in the foreground and am looking straight at the camera, my eyelashes touching my eyebrows and I am thinking, "Excuse me? How dare you interrupt my Daddy and I as we are deep in conversation at this moment."

If this little girl was older she might have been thinking "Can't you see he's talking to me? This Daddy that I love, this Daddy of so few words. Can't you wait until he has finished talking to me?"

My Daddy and me

My family

How long did it take for my mother to come and get me from E.'s house? Days, weeks? Was it because my grandfather objected? I've heard that he said, "This bastard girl does not come into my house." He is a moody person, joking around one day, full of malice against everything and everyone the next. I remember his rage when he searched the garbage and found a toothpaste tube that was not fully empty. But I think that afterwards he regretted what he said about me. Anyway, he was the one who gave me my nickname "Little Macaroon Coffee Bean", which the whole family called me.

I am sure that my grandmother, my Omi, was the one who decided I should be brought there. I can still see her standing in the kitchen with the blue and white Delft tiles – no one has cooked so wonderfully for me – a woman almost six feet tall with an imposing body size. But this body, always dressed in expensive wool suits from Switzerland, is not fat, but firm – and strong as a bear, she is able to move entire cabinets. She can get pretty angry too. Then she furrows her thick black eyebrows and her green eyes light up with fury. My beloved grandmother and her mother, my equally beloved Nana, can have such a loud argument, I think the windows will crack. But I'm not frightened of these two old women, who look like they are about to strangle each other – they actually make me laugh.

I only have good memories of my grandmother, but my mother and her two younger siblings say that she was a humourless, strict and puritanical mother. Their hands were put into bags at night, supposedly so they would not chew their nails. I suspect it was done because of something else so strictly forbidden that you couldn't even mention it.

My grandparents' marriage was a very unhappy one, full of arguments and even violence. Once, as a little girl, my mother saw her father hit her mother so hard she fell to the ground. Horrified, she ran through the garden to the neighbour who was a doctor. She thought that her mother was dead.

Luckily, my mother had someone to console her during her many hardships, her grandmother. Nana lived in Switzerland but often came to Cologne to stay with her only daughter and her family. My mother felt protected when Nana was in the house and remained close to her during her entire life.

Just as my mother, I like my great-grandmother very much. Before my school years, we spend a few weeks in Davos with Nana each year, sometimes even months. When we arrive, the first thing Nana does is open the big chest in the entrance of her house. In my memory, it is filled to the brim with chocolate and other wonderful sweets. And what delicacies there are in Davos! Food which we never see in post-war Germany:

My Mother and Me

Pear bread, air-dried meat, puff-pastries, croissants, crispy bread rolls. Nana's house has double windows that protect from the cold in winter and are covered with frost in the shape of flowers. I have never seen that either. In the summer, I go looking for snails in the garden and lock them in the gap between the two windows. I feed them and give them water and call them my slug colony. Strangely enough, this amuses my Nana. For bedding, instead of a quilt we cover ourselves with a thick, huge, cuddly pillow.

At Nana's house, my mother feels loved and safe, there is no fighting here, and I do not need to live in constant fear of her whims. At home I try to do everything to make her a little happier. In Davos, all is right in the world.

Nana's House in Lyons

The house on Cherry St. in Lyons, NY always felt like home. It was my grandparents' house, Lizetta and Cornelius Collins, my mother's parents. Since my parents and I moved so often, it was the only stable home in my life.When I was 14, I had gone to more than 14 schools. But every summer I would stay for two weeks at the house on Cherry St. The Saratoga sales were the busiest time of the year for my parents. My mother would be at the track trying to get a commission to paint a portrait of a race-horse and my father would be either selling, buying, training, or racing a horse. Now that I think of it, he was also possibly sometimes looking for a job there too. So the first two weeks of August, I stayed with my Nana, Aunt Doll and Uncle Howard. The house in Lyons is a two story, brown shingle Cape Cod style house, similar to the Arts and Crafts or Mission styled houses of the turn of the century with white trim. Sloping 2nd floor ceilings, dark wood, large rooms and decorated with Native American artefacts and portraits of the family painted by my mother. In the small den off of the living room there is a large bear on one wall, on the adjacent wall a bobcat and a badger, above the small fireplace is a deer's head and above the five small windows is a mural that my mother painted of the Colorado that she grew up in. Miners panning for gold, Native Americans and Mexican women washing their clothes in the river, a coach and four making its way west, the general store and their house in the mountains. I loved staying at this house. Every time I went there, it was always the same. Nothing ever changed. It was only later in life, after we had to move to Lyons, did things change.

My grandmother was of German heritage, short, quite stout and she baked cookies, cakes, and pies all the time. Since it was always August when I was there, the yard and all of her roses and other flowers were in full bloom. Hundreds of flowers, irises, gladiolus, pansies, and the roses. Four beautiful beds of roses. The smell of cookies and flowers along with the occasional Raleigh cigarette is what the house in Lyons smelled like. If you went in the cellar you would smell "Kennel #5" because my aunt was a poodle groomer and that's what she sprayed on the dogs just before they were to leave and go home with their owners. Even though I only came for 2 weeks out of each summer and the occasional Christmas, I knew many of the dogs that came. Jacques, Fifi, Buttons, they all came in looking like hell and left looking like show dogs.

As far as grandparents, Nana was the only one I knew. She was my mother's mother. My mother's father, Grandpa Corny died in the 50's before I was born. I have a picture of my father's mother, Nana Rae, holding me as a baby but I suspected that she and my father's father, Grandpa Albert, must have died shortly after I was born because I have no memories of them. None. When I would say my prayers at night, my mother taught me to say, "God bless Nana, Nana Rae, Grandpa Corny, Grandpa Albert, Aunt Doll, Uncle Howard, Mommy and Daddy and me ..." Later in life I would picture each of these people as I recited their names. Nana was a real live moving person, whose image was ever-changing in the prayer, but the other grandparents would be the static images of pictures that I had been shown of them.

Cologne, Germany – 1948
Uncle Harald

We lived with my grandparents for one year, from 1948 to 1949. My mother filed for divorce.

My grandparents had lost their house, the pharmacy and the liquor factory in the bombings. Together with their youngest daughter, my Aunt Ingrid, they survived in the air-raid shelter. Then they found refuge in the countryside, with a friend of my grandfather's. My grandfather had taken precautions and buried away liquor, an excellent bartering object. Like this, the family could survive the famine in the winter of 1945.

In 1948, my grandfather starts up liquor production again. Before the war, he was the well-known producer of Van Munster. The apartment he has rented is big enough to accommodate all of us. Sometimes I go down to the courtyard on my own and watch him work in the barn. A barn full of glass bottles and tubes distilling the liquor, using gas flames. How he is cooking and brewing the liquor on the blue flames reflected by the glass looks so mysterious.

Coca-Cola is about to be re-launched in Germany after the Nazis discredited the German factory as a "Jewish-American company" and closed it without further ado. My grandfather is offered the first new Coca Cola subsidiary, but he actually refuses to produce this "American stuff"!

On December 6, 1948, my grandparents' doorbell rings. Is it Santa Claus? Little "Macaroon" ist told to have a look. I open the door – and am terribly frightened. There is a stranger outside. He looks miserable, even feverish. This picture is still in my mind today. My Omi must have been crying for days with relief, happiness, and pain: her son has come home. But all what happened, as so often in memory, is not pictures but a feeling: the feeling of infinite compassion. Harald has open wounds on his legs, he can not eat, he is so exhausted. He is no longer used to sleeping in a bed and lies down on the bare floor.

Harald is my mother's younger brother. At seventeen, he was drafted by the Third Reich, fought in the Crimea and was captured there by the Russians. For two years, nobody knew if he was dead or alive. My grandmother is said to have gone almost insane with grief.

Now, three years after the end of the war, he finally returns home. He recovers quite quickly, but what he has gone through stays locked inside of him. All he reveals is that he was transferred to a camp in Siberia and made to do forced labor there. The prisoners worked in salt mines where they stood in wet salt to their knees that burned horribly into the open wounds on their legs caused by malnutrition. But Harald doesn't hold any hate for the Russians. The people from the surrounding villages sometimes came to the fence and gave the prisoners food through the mesh wire. Even though, as he knew, they were starving themselves.

This uncle becomes someone between a father and a playmate for me. I have great fun with him and forget about the loss of Aunt Christel which hurts so much. Harald plays with me and jokes around and even builds a radio where you can hear voices from all over the world. But then his mood may suddenly change completely. From one moment to another, he becomes a different person whom I don't understand. How could I have understood? It is beyond my knowledge that the young man's soul is deeply wounded by the war. He calls me "Fifi" like a little puppy and wants me to obey him. And then, the next day he might console me because of my mother's bad mood as she goes through the divorce.

One or two years later – my mother has remarried and we live with her new husband in an own flat – we go to Harald's wedding in St. Gallen. My mother has sewn me a beautiful little dress, a light blue dress made of frilly fabric with a smock. In the church I should have been one of the flower girls, but someone forgot the basket that I was suppose to carry. But wait, I will soon make a grand entrance.

An orchestra plays at the wedding dinner. The bridal couple dances the obligatory waltz. The dance floor fills up, then the orchestra pauses. Suddenly the conductor comes up to me: "Do you want to sing a song, little girl?" I am amazed and do not know what to say. And then I remember a hit from the radio, which I have often heard and sung. Of course, I don't know its name. I sing a few notes. "Do you know this one maybe?" "No, I'm sorry." Well, then it just has to work without music. I'm standing on the dance floor and sing out loudly:

"If men only knew,
how the women are –
Thank goodness, they don't know,
because love makes them blind."

The wedding party bursts out laughing. I am perplexed – why is that so funny? Are they laughing at me?

The dark side of Uncle Harald is associated in my mind with the day when Harald is driving my mother and me somewhere in Grandpa's car. In the pouring rain, the landscape outside is dark. The wipers work like mad, but you can see almost nothing. The car is lurching. I always feel sick whether in a car, a boat, or a train, but this time it's especially bad because my mother and Uncle Harald are nervously smoking during the whole ride. Besides, neither of them tells me a single word about where we are going or why. Finally we get out of the car and go into a hospital. We are taken to a large hall, which is filled with dark brown shelves that reach way up to the ceiling and have drawers with white name tags like in a pharmacy. Here, all sorts of different instruments are used in order to measure me: my nose, my ears, the distance between my eyes and more. It is an endless procedure. Does that mean that I am sick? Of course, I have no idea that these are tests which have to do with a paternity suit. I don't even know what a paternity suit is. Anyway, something is wrong with me, I'm sure of that.

Up and Down the East Coast – 1963–1968

Puttin' on the Ritz

I definitely didn't have a normal childhood by anyone's standards, but it was normal to me. We followed the track. Saratoga, Aqueduct, Belmont, in NY. Monmouth in NJ, Pimlico and Laurel in Maryland, Keeneland in Kentucky, then onto Gulfstream and Hialeah in Florida. My perception of the world is, I think, pretty different from other people because of the way I was raised. And strangely enough, I've never been a big gambler because of my life growing up on the track. I saw too many people betting their money away. There was one woman I would see each year at Saratoga, she was a person that we didn't see off of the track, but a friend never the less. Each year we would stop and talk with her. She was always sitting outside, always had the racing form beside her and a racing program in her hand. She was older than my parents, and really always nice to me. She would ask me what horse I liked in the next race, like if my advice was something to listen to. One year when we came back she wasn't there. We didn't even have to ask if she had died, we knew. If she wasn't on the track, she was dead.

I also saw the richest people in the world at that time and they were some of the saddest. Of course there were those who owned the horses and they weren't really gambling. Their lives and livelihood were not even riding on the backs of the horses because they had so much money, made in other ways, or passed down from their families that horse racing was more a hobby or sport, rather than an income maker as it is today. These names mean less today, but in 1963 they were the creme de la creme of old money, and the heart of the racing world royalty: Ashlyn Cannon, Louisa DuPont Carpenter,

Jock Whitney, Paul Mellon, Alfred Vanderbilt and the stars that hung around them like Don Ameche and Tallulah Bankhead.

From this time I remember highlights, things that impressed me greatly. Like riding in the back of Alfred Vanderbilt's Silver Streak Rolls Royce; flying in Louisa's private plane; answering the phone and telling my mother that it was "Tallulah, darling …"

They were individualistic, fascinating people. I understood that I should act different with these people. To smile, say please and thank you. Put my napkin on my lap and only interject one or maybe two sentences into a conversation, then smile and say thank you again. Oh, and order steak. My father taught me that when I go to a restaurant to not order pork chops, order steak. Eat Pork chops at home, he would say.

For a kid, I saw some pretty bizarre occurrences when we were puttin' on the ritz. Like the family who lived next door to us, maybe in Florida. My parents would go over to their house for parties. We would see this family once for a month or so every year. One year we heard a commotion the morning after a party and looking out the front door saw the "paddy wagon" parked in front of the neighbor's house. Next thing we see is the wife being brought out in a straight jacket screaming and laughing her head off.

"What's wrong with Mrs. – , Mommy?"

"Oh, it looks like she had too much to drink last night," says my mother.

But nothing screams puttin' on the ritz like having your very own racehorse. When my parents bought Yankee Blaze he was not a yearling, he was an older horse and he had run before. I don't think he won very much, but my father and mother saw something in the horse and they purchased it. The official owner was Ann Collins Evans and the Trainer was Laramie G. Evans.

The memory is one that never becomes less vivid as the years pass on. Just thinking of it can bring me to tears of joy instantly. My mother is on my left and my father on the right. I am in the middle as always. We are sitting in the stands at Pimlico Race track, in a private box. Our horse is led into the gate with the other horses. The race is a mile and a quarter. The bell goes off, the gates open, the horses lunge out, and "They're off!" The announcer begins to call the race in his sing song way and every time he names our horse, it's the last name called. I look up at my father, way up because it is 1963 and I am a "peanut" and he is so very, very tall.

"Daddy, he's last ..."

"Shhh ... It's okay Larry Ann ..."

I watch some more and they round the first post.

"... and Yankee Blaze trailing behind."

"Daddy, he's last!"

"It's okay, he'll be fine."

My mother on my left is intently watching the race, silent.

I turn my attention to the race as the horses round the far side of the track. It seems like there is a little less distance between Yankee Blaze and the rest of the horses now.

"But Daddy, he's last ..."

"Shhhh, watch the race, he'll make his move."

I hear my mother start to snap her finger. She's a snapper when hoping a horse will win, her right hand starts at shoulder height and heads toward the direction of her lap, with a loud "SNAP" of her fingers on the way down.

"Come on, Yankee Blaze ..." She snaps again.

I look at the race and the horses are about to round the 3/4 of a mile point and that horse of ours starts to really move. I mean it is overtaking the horse ahead of it, and then the horse ahead of that one ... and ...

"Come on, Yankee Blaze ..." She snaps.

My father is a leg hitter. He uses his large hand to hit the side of his leg or the program in his hand to hit the side of his leg when he is trying to will a horse to go faster.

"Come on, Yankee Blaze ..." He hits.

My eyes are glued on the horse and the three of us start to stand. That horse is literally flying now, overtaking one, then another, then another horse.

The horses round the mile-post and the crowd begins to roar, everyone for his own bet or horse. My parents are not screaming, or yelling, but they are intense.

Snap, hit, "Come on, Yankee Blaze, come on!"

I start my own chant right along with them. The roar of the crowd is deafening because the underdog, the long shot is now breaking away from the pack and is in the lead.

Come on Yankee Blaze! Come on!

Larry, Ann and Larry
Ann with Yankee Blaze
in the Winners' Circle

He pulls further away from the pack and now no one can catch this horse, it is on fire! The sound of the horses' hoofs on the track and the roar of the crowd is deafening.

Yankee Blaze shoots across the finish line way ahead of any of the horses!

"He won! He Won!! HE WON!!

My father takes my hand, and we run out of the box and down to the winner's circle. Me! In the winner's circle with the photographer and the flowers around the horses neck and my parents, radiant. Yankee Blaze broke the track record at Pimlico for a Mile and a Quarter that day and held that record for twenty years, until 1983.

My father bred and trained thoroughbreds and my mother was an artist of racehorses." I don't think I really understood just how unusual that was.

Mother's Second and Third Marriage

The SS. Hitler's personal paramilitary organisation who executed civilians, tortured and murdered prisoners of war, and drove millions of human beings out or sent them to the gas chambers. A SS officer of the Third Reich was my mother's second husband. She married him in 1950.

A. is a lawyer and has just opened an office. However, he could not do that under his own name: he had not been convicted, but for a lawyer, a past with the SS was unacceptable. I do not like A. He is a huge man who beats our dog and scares me. Worst of all are his big nostrils, which look incredibly brutal. He is not good to my mother! The terrible arguments between my mother and him often wake me in the middle of the night. More than once she pulls me out of bed, throws my coat over my nightgown and flees with me through the city park to her parents. One night I'm so desperate I try to call the police while they are beating each other. I'm five years old and can dial the emergency number, but I can not tell the officer on the phone what street I live on. The screaming adults, the sounds of furniture breaking, a chair falling over – the official hears it, but he can't do anything for me.

Why did my mother get involved with A. and marry him? I still don't understand it. She had no sympathy for the Nazis. She even knew what it felt like to be a victim, as she had often been considered a Jew, because of her Mediterranean looks. Once, the other passengers even threw her out of a tram. Didn't she know that a man like A. would not shed his brutality from one day to the next like a glove? Or was this just a fatal attraction? The tragic compulsion to repeat the marriage of her parents?

There is a huge baroque cabinet in our living room where she keeps glasses, sweets and liquor. More and more often, I see her sneaking a drink directly from the bottle. I feel so vulnerable.

I have a memory from this time that is stamped on my mind. My mother is sitting at her desk, bent over piles of paper. She sighs and starts to cry. I want to comfort her and know why she is crying.

"I can't tell you."

The answer makes me worried and I want to know even more.

"Please, please, tell me!"

Finally, she says only one sentence that silences me: "It's because of you."

There it is again, the feeling that I am to blame. But for what, what have I done? I live in constant fear that she will become even more desperate or angry and will not love me anymore.So I try to be as quiet as a mouse and hope that she'll get into a better mood again. But not always. Sometimes I get my revenge. As she always wants to be in the spotlight while I seem to be invisible, one day I take hold of the scissors and go to her closet. I cut all of her clothes to the same length. This is the one and only time my mother spanks me. She uses a wire-braided carpet beater. Afterwards we are both in tears. She says she's sorry. Today I know that my mother's moods were also due to the paternity suit. And I don't remember her as being bad tempered all the time. There are times when she is very nice and tender. Then I'm her "one and only". How I wish there was some sort of escape from these ups and downs – a father who would always, always love me!

I am told to call my mother's husband, A., "Papi". My "real dad" – that's how my mother calls E. – we see once a month.

We are always picked up in the Cadillac by his chauffeur. On the first day of school children are always given a bag of sweets by their parents. But E. doesn't buy me the bag, he tells his chauffeur to do it. There is a picture I have that shows me holding on tight to this bag of sweets. My good grades are the only thing E. seems to appreciate about me.

"You've inherited his intelligence," my mother always says. I don't want to hear that, I do not want to have inherited anything from E.

During the divorce, the court ordered E. to pay a handsome amount in alimony payments for my upbringing. Astonishingly, E. is not upset about this, on the contrary, he and my mother are happy to see each other when they meet once a month at a local restaurant. But they don't seem to notice me. I could just as well have joined the dog under the table. At the end of the meetings, my mother always got an envelope, the check for my maintenance.

In 1955 there is a new turn in our lives. I'm nine. My mother divorces A. At thirty-five, she is still a beautiful, expressive woman, slender and elegant. All the men start flirting with her immediately and she marries a third time. She is very much in love with Paul. He is very good-looking, always well dressed, has traveled a lot and has gentlemanlike manners. My mother is carried away by him and he no less by her. Now, finally, everything is wonderful, I am convinced of that.

Paul's father was a lawyer and Jewish. During the last two years of the war, he and his family had to live undercover. His parents hid in a convent, and he and his sister lived with friends who risked their lives by hiding them. By the end of the war, they were living in bombed-out houses.

After the war, Paul focused on his career. All he wanted was security. Like all Nazi victims, he received compensation from the federal government, which together with every extra penny of his salary he invested in the stock market. In the years of the German economic boom one could make a fortune this way. Now, at thirty-seven, he was ready to get married.

For me, this marriage means that again, a new "daddy" comes into my life. We move into a beautiful, large apartment overlooking the city park. For the first time, I have a room of my own.

It has a nice bright green carpet. My favourite piece of furniture is the wicker chair, where I can sit and read for hours, our new doggie curled up in my lap. In 1956, my little brother D. is born, making Paul incredibly happy. I have always longed for siblings and for years put pieces of sugar on the windowsill for the stork who brings the babies. Now he has finally listened to my wish!

Everything Will be Fine.
Marion and Brother

Larry: Married Once, Married Twice, Married Thrice

My mother, who is in heaven I am sure, wouldn't be too happy that I'm writing about Daddy's first and second wife. She was as possessive of him as I am. But since I know very little about both of these women, I'm sure she won't be too mad.

Daddy first married in 1942. Right before he went to the war. There were a lot of marriages that happened right as the GI was signing up. It must have been very consoling for the soldiers to have someone waiting for them at home. Problem was, this was no short war. So waiting for your GI to come home, took years.

My father told me that he received a "Dear John" letter in the war from his first wife M. Sadly, many American wives sent such letters to end their relationships with their soldiers overseas. It seems that after the war, they tried to make things work, because my half brother, B., was born.

For years after I found out about B. I tried to get daddy to call him. But he wouldn't. Another of his expressions was "You can't go back, never look back." But this was a child, not an old home. In 1991, my parents had come over to Spain for my wedding and I can't remember who called who, but I had my father's son on the phone and my father sitting on the couch behind me.

"Daddy. B. is on the phone. Why don't you talk to him."

(Pause.)

"Oh, he doesn't want to talk to me."

"Yes, he does."

Well he finally took the phone and they talked. It was probably awkward and probably stilted, but they talked. At that time, B.'s mother was still alive. She passed away about 10 years later of cancer. She had married again, and B. had family from that union.

B. and my father met sometime the next year in Buffalo, NY and I think that they had a good time talking about many things, including baseball, a huge passion for them both.

I know even less about Daddy's second wife, H. H. was from Wisconsin. I have no idea how she and Daddy met, but they married in Dade County, Florida in 1949. Daddy said she came from money and maybe he was blinded by that, because he failed to notice that she was an alcoholic. He said that her family did their best to hide it from him. Strangely enough they were married for seven years. H.'s father, D. was the Vice President of a bank and Manager of a large business in Wisconsin. Daddy said that he was offered a job laying out a new community, figuring out where the streets would be and planning the development of this community.I always got the impression that he really wanted that marriage to work out because he liked the job so much. It seems H. and my father were going to live in Lexington, Kentucky on a horse farm she was purchasing, But finally, H. got "returned to sender" because their marriage ended.

Cologne, Germany – 1960

The Moment of Truth

"It won't work again."

I will never forget the desperation in my mother's eyes as she says this sentence to me.

She feels trapped. She thought that with Paul, who was such a cheerful person, she would live an interesting life. She thought that they would travel, throw parties, and go out a lot, but since he now has a family, he rather likes to be at home and play with his little son after work. Then, in 1959, my mother gives birth to another baby, our little sister L. Raising children was not something that made my mother happy. I'm in tears. This family was our last hope! Of course I notice that my mother has changed after my little brother's birth and that now there is a lot of fighting in the house. But why is everything falling apart again? Why is my mother never satisfied? Paul hires a lot of domestic help for her – a nanny, a maid who serves the food and clears the table when you press a button under the carpet, and a cleaning lady. But taking care of a big household with toddlers is too much for her. She has always been a heavy smoker, and she now drinks regularly. She often loses her temper with the small children. Sometimes she will get so upset that I come to her aid and spank the children for her. I still feel guilty about it today. Of course I'm jealous of my little siblings, but I do not confess that to anybody or even to myself. And no one asks me about it.

The regular meetings with E. have stopped, we barely see him any more. He has also remarried and that causes a new problem. E.'s new wife doesn't understand why he's paying alimony for a child who may not be his own. He stops the payments, and my mother gets a lawyer and goes to court. So the question of paternity is raised a second time.

I am fourteen years old when my mother finally tells me her secret: At the end of the war down in Munich with Inge and her mother, she says, there was an American officer with whom she had "a relationship". Soon after, E. came to visit. Therefore, when she got pregnant, either man could possibly be the father. The medical tests that were made on me in 1948, however, showed "almost certainly" that E. was my father. She says I should not worry and please, please not judge her because of the affair.

I'm not listening anymore. I'm speechless. The ground under my feet breaks away, as does any trust in my mother. It seems as if a stranger were sitting in front of me. So that's finally the explanation for the measurements of my ears, nose, eyes that were made when I was a little girl! This disturbing memory comes rushing back. At the same time, I know that my mother isn't describing it right. In biology class we learned that with the methods available at the time – there were no DNA tests – it wasn't possible to positively identify a person as the father. One could only, if both men were present, with a bit of luck exclude one of them. But I do not tell my mother. I suppose she knows that, too. Is she lying to me on purpose? Or does she want to give me a false sense of security? I don't ask. I don't cry, I don't scream. I also don't tell my mother that what she revealed to me, as shocking as it is, at least has something positive about it: I would be glad if E. were not my father.

What also stays in my mind about this moment of truth: my mother is a lot more concerned about herself than about me, about whether I am condemning her morally or not. She is ashamed of her affair. I don't even think about such old-fashioned moral standards, and in this moment I don't care at all about what she thinks about herself. I'm concerned about me, as all of a sudden I have become a stranger to myself.

I'm not who I thought I was and I have no idea who the other one is. I also feel shame, but it's not my mother's shame. Do my grandfather's words come back to mind? "This bastard girl doesn't come into my house?" Did I hear him saying that myself? I don't think so. But then, who told me this monstrosity?

12 | Larry Ann
Brewster, New York – 1968/1969
The German Girl

My mother was sitting in her white chair in the living room. The white chair with no arm rests. My father was walking through or in the room. I seem to have been in the open dining room attached to the living room. Papers are involved, paperwork, and they were talking about someone needing to receive some money. I asked what they were talking about and

my mother said that these people in Germany were trying to say that daddy was the father of a girl there. In order for the girl to receive the money, your father had to say that he wasn't her father. For some reason I can't remember asking "What child? "When?" "Really" or "HUH?" I just remember going "Oh." and going on my merry way. Sometimes I wonder if I'm retarded.

Many years later in Lyons, as I was cleaning out my parents drawers after their deaths I came across a letter from my Grandma Rae to my father dated from May 1st, 1958.

'May 1st 1958

Dear Larry:

We received your letter today and I immediately phoned B. He is nursing a sprained ankle and will be out of school for two weeks. The doctor advised him to be off the foot entirely. He was trying out the "Little League." This will of course exclude him for which I am grateful. Dad thinks he is a little too young.

I am writing this note to you to tell you to be careful. A detective agency by name LaSalle in Chicago is on your trail. They phoned several times trying to get information as to your whereabouts. I have

Nana Rae's letter

She talks about B., his sprained ankle, how well he is doing in school, but then goes on:

69

(...) I am writing this note to you to tell you to be careful. A detective agency by name La Salle in Chicago is on your trail. They phoned several times trying to get information as to your whereabouts. I have at no time given them any information whatever. Both a man and a woman phoned. She said she would like to come out and see me. I told her I couldn't see her and wished she would stop calling. They called dad at his office and he told them not to call again. These people who have detectives on your trail – this is not the first time. Some years back they were in Chicago as I understand they are now. They are from Germany and told me what the trouble was about. (...)

When I read that letter, I fantasized that my father was working as an undercover agent in Germany, a spy of some sort. What else could it be if there were Germans on your trail in 1958 so long after the war? There are tons of spy flicks where the man or woman lived what seemed a normal life, playing golf, living in small towns, going to PTA meetings, when in reality he was a spy, working to bring freedom to the oppressed people of totalitarian regimes and feeding intel to his home country.

I always seem to find these things in drawers. These drawers are like a metaphor in my life because I was never given anything on top of the table, in clear view. I always had to find it for myself in all of these drawers. They contained years and years of history and secrets.

Well, I would never know if my father was leading a double life, so the letter went back in the drawer and I'm not really sure if I connected it at all in my subconscious mind to "the German Girl."

Paul

E. has organised a detective bureau to track down Larry and finally settle the question of fatherhood. The detectives have done a good job. E. has called Larry, with my mother and the lawyers present (she only tells me this part of the story years later). Larry is prepared to come to Europe and undergo a paternity test. But when the receiver is passed on to my mother, she refuses to talk to him. She doesn't want the two men to meet, and she doesn't want forensic medicine to settle which one of them is my father.

Fate has caught up with my mother completely unexpectedly. There is no other option than to confess her story to Paul, her third husband. She has not told him about this episode in her – in our – life. But Paul reacts in a way that my mother never expected. He does not condemn her. Taking the moral high ground is contrary to his way of thinking and feeling. He takes a pragmatic approach and advises her to avoid yet another paternity suit with an uncertain outcome. What if Laramie Evans is confirmed to be my father? Would he be able to support me financially? Would he be willing to do that after so many years?

I still remember sitting on the green sofa in our living room. Paul offers to adopt me! I am completely thrown off guard. This is the most generous offer thinkable. But what would this mean? Bearing Paul's surname? Every part of me resists that thought. It would just be yet another lie. No! I am certain: I don't want to be adopted. I mercilessly point out the adults' contradictions. They ask us not to lie but shamelessly lie to us. My mother has lied to me for fourteen years, so she is no longer an authority for me. But Paul still is. But given that I'm in the midst of my adolescence, I am in opposition to everyone: the teachers at school, but above all Paul. Like him, I do not believe in God, but because he is such an ardent atheist, I want to be confirmed. I am also for social justice, but because he defends the Social Democrats with all their inner contradictions, I start to hate them and their forever shouting chairman Erich Ollenhauer. And because Paul gives my younger brother and sister great amounts of freedom, I am of the opinion that they should be taught limits. With all this in mind, how could I say yes to his offer to adopt me? Years later, after I have flown the coop and married, Paul and I become very close. I feel like I'm his daughter, and shortly before he dies I tell him in a long and fulfilling conversation how much I owe him. But none of us ever mentioned the adoption again. I had forgotten the episode, and it has only recently resurfaced in my memory. But now it's too late. It is terrible how death makes all missed opportunities so final. I can't ask Paul any more if I hurt him back then, or if he understood how I felt.

The trial against E. ends with a settlement. He agrees to pay me a severance payment, which will satisfy any further claims. The sum is peanuts for him. For me, the money is enough to finance my living costs and my education.

From the outside, nothing changes. I continue to be seen as the daughter of Dr. E., the lawyer from Cologne. The last time I see him is about one year after the trial. He invites my mother and me to his new house, where he lives with his new wife – a luxurious property in a prime location. His wife wants to humiliate us, and proudly shows us the whole house, her empire, which is furnished like a castle. We sit down to eat. The mood is tense, and the alcohol is flowing freely. The four people sitting at this table and eating dinner all know the truth: the question of who my father is was never settled during the trial. By midnight, E. and my mother are so drunk that neither of them can stand any longer. When we are finally ready to go home, I refuse to sit in the car with my mother, given the state she is in.

"I want the chauffeur to drive us home!"

"Don't make such a scene. I'm perfectly capable of driving a car."

"Don't be silly – your mother can drive."

"I'm not driving with you!"

By now, I am screaming, but nobody is helping me. I then throw all of my fourteen-year-old self onto the beautiful Persian carpet and throw a huge tantrum, insisting that I will not take one step out of this house. In the end, E.'s wife caves in and wakes up the chauffeur.

E. died not long after. We don't go to his funeral.

13 | Larry Ann
The East Coast – 1959–1968

Larry & Ann, The Story of My Parents

'Heads would turn' when Larry and Ann would walk through the crowds in Saratoga. These two tall, beautiful people were charming and looked like movie stars. But heads turned because it was more than just beauty, I think it was because people could feel the love that they had for each other. It radiated off of them.

Larry had been married twice before and Ann once before. They found each other later in life, when Larry was forty-three and Ann was forty-two. Larry was working for the Thorough-

bred Record as a writer and he was to write an article about Ann Collins, the artist of racehorses. Ann was famous in the equine art world as she had by that time painted the winners of many very famous races like Alsab beating Whirlaway, commissioned by Albert Sabath and some very famous horses such as Citation commissioned by Alfred Vanderbilt. The funny part is that Larry never finished the article. They fell in love. It was the kind of love you hear about in storybooks. They never fought, they said "I Love You" before every drink

Larry and Ann

and they kissed all the time. Even in public. Larry would do anything for Ann and Ann would do anything for Larry. They loved each other more than anything in this whole world. Sometimes, I felt, even more than me.

Larry and Ann had me, Larry Ann, in 1960 in Spring Lakes, NJ on a farm called Chasmar. My mother never had any children with her first husband. She told me that doctors had told her she couldn't have any. Larry always said "It took a mighty powerful man to get your mother pregnant!" Really no one knew she was pregnant. She always had an 18 inch waist and when I was born in her seventh month of pregnancy it probably wasn't any bigger than 24 inches. With the billowing skirts she wore her lower abdomen was pretty well hidden. The night she had me she was out dancing with Larry. Her water broke in the bathroom and she said she thought it was time to go to the hospital.

Since my mother had to follow the racing season in order to get commissions for paintings, Daddy switched professions and began training and later breeding racehorses. My earliest memories are the smell of horse manure and turpentine.

Their love for each other was so strong that it didn't matter if they had money or not. From 1960 – 1968 we moved constantly. Each year we traveled from Monmouth all the way to Miami and all the racetracks in between. After a year stint in Tenino, Washington in 1969 we moved to Brewster where we stayed five whole years.

America I

So my father is American. Or is this just wishful thinking on my part? I can't be sure of anything. But Laramie Evans is no stranger to me. I've always wanted to know who the man with the big eyebrows is in my mother's photo album. And one thing is certain: it would be exciting to have an American father.

Like all teenagers, I am very much into the "new music" from America, which our parents find awful: Cliff Richard, Bill Haley, Eartha Kitt and, of course, Elvis Presley. I swoon over Clark Gable. But I'm not allowed to go to the cinema to see "Gone With the Wind", as I'm far from being eighteen. Like all teenagers, I drink Coca Cola and say "okay". But we are not even aware of the extent to which this youth culture from the United States is invading Europe. The Germans, in particular, admire America, which has given them the Marshall Plan (some would even taunt Germany as the 49th American state). John F. Kennedy is more popular than any German politician, and his death in 1963 is mourned by the whole world.

At my school, I watch a group of high school graduates dance Rock 'n' Roll. They learned it in America, when they were "over there" as part of a student exchange programme. I am seized by the rhythm, the girls' enthusiasm is contagious, and I am completely awestruck by their acrobatic efforts, as they whirl each other through the air. I am now also determined to go to school in the United States for a year. But there is one thing I did not expect: you are not guaranteed to come back to your old class after spending one year away. When I find out about this, I bury my plans. Having to retake the year spent in America would mean having to stay at home one more year. And that would be unbearable.

Our home has turned into hell. My mother and Paul argue every day. She is already drunk by lunchtime. My smaller siblings are as helpless as I am. Our employees are constantly quitting, as nobody can stand being at our place for a long time. Do I hate my mother for making us go through all this? Is only she to blame for this situation? I don't think so, and I can't get myself to hate her either. She is plagued by an abysmal despair, and sometimes she cries as bitterly as no human being should ever cry. She cries about the injustice her parents have done to her, the injustice her men have done to her – she cries about her failed life. With this in mind, I feel only infinite compassion.

They Lie About their Ages

In Brewster we lived on a horse farm called Tilly Foster Stock Farm. In the five years that we lived there, my father turned the place around from a boarding stable to a farm that bred some pretty damn good horses that sold well at the Saratoga sales. I remember him working in his office on the farm during breeding season. One cigarette burning in the ashtray, one behind his ear and one about to be lit.

When my friends came over to play with me on the farm there were always things to do. There are miles and miles of woods and fields where a person could get lost, but we don't. There are two large barrels that drip molasses that sometimes we let drip on our fingers and lick. Our house is on a hill and out of my bedroom window you can see a fantastic view of Middle Branch Reservoir.

I remember a day when My friend K. and I are playing in the house. Maybe we are about 11 or 12 years old. Luckily I'm not trying to start a bonfire in the basement like another time she came over. K. and I are in the dining room and we are somehow on the subject of our parent's ages. Hers are 38 and 39 and I say mine are older, I think. They told me 40 or 42, I can't remember.

"Look on their license." K. says. "See when they were born."

I look in my mother's purse and find her wallet. I find the license and pull it out.

"1916 ... so she's ..." I never was any good at math.

"She's fifty-five."

"No she's not."

"Yes she is."

I think this was the first thing that my parents fibbed about. Not really a lie, stretching the truth, I'd say because they really did not look that old. Later they said that they hadn't told me their real ages because they thought I would tell someone and they would not be able to get jobs, being so old.

I think that was the year my father had the heart attack. I guess people thought that he was kind of young to have a heart attack, but I knew he wasn't.

15 | Marion
Zurich, Switzerland – 1965
America II

I see a girl standing at Zurich main station looking a bit lost. She is obviously American, a mix of Grace Kelly and Marilyn Monroe. She approaches me and asks for directions. Me, an introverted and shy 19-year-old. I have left home and moved here a month ago. So far, I have spent my time reading books by Lake Zurich in the autumn sun. Books on existentialism and the psychology of alcoholism. To my own astonishment, I spontaneously say:

"Come, let's have a cup of coffee together!"

Linda and I become the closest of friends in no time. For days and nights, we explain our worlds to each other, which in those days looked much more different than they do to-day. Her carefree nature and her boundless and quintessentially American optimism make her seem a bit naive in my eyes, but I let her enthusiasm carry me away. Linda takes a break from her trip through Europe for half a year and stays in Zurich.

I have enrolled both at drama school and the university at the same time. My favourite subject of Theatre Studies is not taught in Zurich, so I plan to move on after one term.

I get to know **him** in the university cafeteria. I am sitting at a table with Linda and her boyfriend, and a dazzlingly good-looking student with a fashionable beard sits down at the table next to ours. Linda's boyfriend tells us about his hitch-hiking adventures and about being picked up by an elderly lady.

"You won't believe it, but she tried to hit on me!"

I have to laugh out so loud that it resonates throughout the entire hall. (Today, at almost sixty, I don't find this story at all funny). I can't stop laughing, and lo and behold, the young man with the beard looks at me amused. This gives me a reason to smile at him apologetically the next day.

Volker admits to me later that his circle of friends had been discussing which one of us was cuter: the blonde or the black-haired girl. For him, there was no question ... He grew up in the Ruhr Basin, not far from Cologne. He took part in peace marches and, as is the right of every German, he refused to do military service as a conscientious objector. He is studying sociology. I admire that. Even though I was shaped politically by the leftist/liberal views of Paul, I was never politically active. Now, many of our discussions revolve around politics. Unlike Linda, Volker and I are convinced that the Vietnam War is a great act of injustice.

In its review of 1965, the television news programme of the German broadcaster shows a shocking segment.

"For the first time, the US Air Force has used napalm bombs, which create fires with temperatures of more than 2000 degrees Celsius. At the start of the year, the United States had roughly 23,500 soldiers in Vietnam, by the end of the year this number has increased

The US used Napalm bombs in Vietnam

to nearly 200,000. In South Vietnam, Air Marshal Ki becomes the head of a military government. He declares Hitler as a role model. The South Vietnamese army recruits children and trains them to fight. As a result of the bombings, the first student demonstrations against the Vietnam War take place."

81

When Linda returns to the United States, her mind about the Vietnam War has changed.

Three years later, in 1969, she returns to Zurich. On 21 July, there is a more glorious America to admire: American astronauts are the first human beings to land on the moon. Together, we see the astronauts hoist the Stars and Stripes and are overcome with joy. As always, we talk about everything under the sun.

But there is one thing I never tell my American friend: the story about Larry. Today, I don't understand why I kept it to myself. Was I too ashamed to admit it to Linda? Was I still haunted by the idea of being a 'bastard child'?

Volker and I decide to get married. Much to the amusement of all our friends, who are not in the least bit interested in tying the knot so early. But we are on cloud nine, and my first great love gives me a lot of self-confidence. I want to hold on to the fortune that fell into my lap.

My mother is completely against this early marriage. When I don't yield, she becomes enraged.

"Love," she says, "what is love? It'll be gone after two years anyway. And then you'll realise what a stupid thing you've done."

These are the words of a disillusioned forty-six-year-old, whose life has only given her disappointments. What do I have in common with her? If anything, the fighting with her convinces me that I'm doing the right thing. On September 29, 1967, we get married. Just one year later, we would have probably thought twice about it. But for entirely different reasons than my mother thought of! Within one year, the world has changed. We live in a commune with other students, and political revolution and free sex are the order of the day.

"Are you married? Forget it! "

"Are you jealous? What a bourgeois sentiment!"

Everyone in the world smokes weed – apart from me; it makes me depressed. There are protests at the university and on the streets. I read Marx and Mao and become enthusiastic about Summerhill's theories of anti-authoritarian education. A member of our commune founds the first gay club in Zurich. But for me, the biggest discovery is definitely the women's movement. And from women's liberation there is a straight path to the general elimination of injustice. That is our task! Fathers? At best, they show some understanding, like Paul, who gets involved with Amnesty International. Otherwise, they are part of the authorities we are fighting. Inheritance? Inheritance, for us, is connected to an ideology that upholds "blood and soil", which has caused infinite suffering and is deeply repugnant. The human being is a product of its social environment. Period. I therefore forget about the topic of fatherhood.

In the eyes of many left-wing comrades, however, we are no more than "champagne socialists". The house we live in is located directly next to Lake Zurich, in the rich municipality of Küsnacht, albeit in a run-down house. We have a tennis court and a boathouse, and we throw parties with two hundred guests, strobe lighting and a buffet. I buy a sports car and nice clothes. All of this is paid for with the money I had received from E. We keep on spending it generously, the rest Volker loses on the stock markets, and ultimately nothing is left of it. Was it pure cockiness – or was there something inside me that wanted to get rid of the money? Did I have the feeling that it wasn't really mine?

Volker and I gift each other our first trip to the United States in 1972, after I finish my university degree. I will never forget our incredulous amazement as we step out of Grand Central Station onto the street and find ourselves in the midst of sky-scrapers. The sheer size of the country is overwhelming too, and we criss-cross it in Greyhound buses. Everywhere we find the same language and culture, the same friendly manners, the same underlying optimism, which is slowly disappearing on our old continent. But what is completely alien to us is the divide between whites and blacks. During the six-week journey, we don't get to know a single African-American.

In 1973, I visit my mother, who has meanwhile separated from her third husband Paul and has joined me in Switzerland, settling down in the place where she was always happy: Davos. Cécile, a friend from the commune, accompanies me part of the way. We drive along the deep-blue Walensee Lake. There is something mysterious about it, something almost sinister, given the way it is surrounded by tall, rugged mountains that nearly drop down into the water. Above it is a mountain pass, and during the trip I open up to Cécile and tell her the story of my many fathers. Cécile listens with affection, and her reaction is clear:

"You have to talk to your mother about it! You are both living under false pretences. She pretends that E. is your father. Or she even believes it. And you pretend to believe it too. This misunderstanding has always stood between the two of you!"

Cécile is right – what she says makes sense to me. But how should I tackle this topic with my mother? How could I have the conversation with her that I refused to have when I was fourteen, and to which none of us has ever returned?

But somehow I find the courage. I expect my mother to ward everything off or even get angry. But to my biggest surprise, she listens to me. It is as if she has been waiting for it and as if she knew that I suspected Laramie Evans was my father. She responds to my longings and my fears. And then the bomb drops: she gives me the letters from Larry. The love letters he wrote in 1949, which until then I did not know existed. Letters that make me cry. I have never had a father carry me in his arms, I have never sat on the lap of a father – and here is a man who writes: *"Marion is such a darling, and I see a lot of you when I look at the pictures of her. I certainly love her, as she is a part of me."*

After everything is revealed, my mother and I grow so much closer, as close as we had only been early in my childhood. She even lets herself be persuaded to write to Larry. We send the letter to the address where he could be reached during the second paternity suit – which is now thirteen years ago. Chasmar Farm, a farm for thoroughbred horses.

1973

Dear Larry,

you will be surprised to hear from me after so many years have passed. I have been often thinking of you and wondering how you are. I could never forget those weeks when we knew each other. The reason why I am writing to you today is that a couple of days ago I had a very intimate talk with Marion. I realized for the first time how much she is concerned about the question who is her father.

I divorced from Ernst Hölscher in 1949. He is dead since a few years. Between Marion and him there could never develop a personal relation. She knew that Ernst Hölscher would not acknowledge her as his daughter, I did not want to trouble your life with all the circumstances I had to go through and which were sometimes desperate for me. I thought the most important for me to do in this situation was to protect Marion and let her grow up happy. This is why we never started talking about our love in a more concrete way.

Marion is 27 years old by now. She studied and finished with a PhD, like her husband to whom she is married since six years. They both live in Zurich, she works for the television and Volker at the university.

I live in Switzerland, too, since I separated from my husband eight years ago. I have two more children who still go to a boarding school in Germany. They always come to spend their holidays in Davos.

I hope very much this letter will reach you. Marion helped me to write it. I would be very happy to get an answer from you. Marion told me she had always had feelings for you – she knew you from your pictures that I always kept and from what I told her about our time in Unterhaching. I believe it would have a great meaning for the three of us if we could find out the truth. If this is also your feeling after so many years, we will be ready to come over to see you. It would make me very glad.

Letter to Larry Evans

Dear Larry,
You will be surprised to hear from me after so many years have passed. I have been often thinking of you and wondering how you are. I could never forget these weeks when we knew each other. The reason why I am writing to you today is that a couple of days ago I had a very intimate talk with Marion. I realized for the first time how much she is concerned about the question who is her father. (...)

Larry Ann
Brewster, New York – 1973
The Argument

I never saw my parents fight except once. It was about 1973.
At that time things were already turbulent with Larry's job at
Tilly Foster. Another worker on the farm was trying to cut out
Larry as the middleman breeding and selling horses and even
though he had another five year contract in place he was soon
to be fired. He must have already seen the writing on the wall.
I can imagine he was pretty worried that he might have to look
for a new job at 59 years of age.

It sticks in my mind only because it was an argument between
these two people that never fought, but really I remember very
little about it. I remember raised voices. I seem to remember
"Don't be stupid, Ann!" That may or may not have been said.
What I do remember is my mother storming out of the house,
car keys clutched in her hand, blond hair on fire and my father sitting in his chair. I remember looking at him just sitting
there.

   "She's leaving!!"
   "No she's not."
   The car started.
   "Go after her, Daddy! She's leaving!!"
   "No, she's not."
   "Yes, she is!"

I remember him finally getting up from his chair. He must
have gone out to stop her from leaving because the memory
stops there. I always thought it was about my teeth because my
mother told me that that was the only argument they ever had,
over my teeth. She wanted me to get braces and my father said
they would straighten by themselves. Well I got braces. But
this argument that I remember was just too volatile, too raw
and heartbreaking to be over something as trivial as braces.

Chaos

The letter to Laramie Evans, Chasmar Farm, is returned – address unknown. In February 1974, we send it to the Spring Lake municipal administration and the police station with a request to forward the letter to Mr. Evans. But we wait in vain. We neither hear back from the authorities nor from Laramie Evans. Did he not receive the letter, or doesn't he want to answer? We will never know.

Of course, today I ask myself why on earth I never wrote to him myself. Maybe I would have had a chance. Didn't I think of the possibility that Laramie Evans was likely to be married and have a family, and therefore might have been willing to meet me, but not my mother? The true answer is that I simply didn't have the courage. Was he really my father? Now, I had to come to terms with the disappointment about the fact that there was still no answer to this question.

Did I think back then that I might have a brother named Barry, who was one year younger than me? The small boy who Larry wrote about in his letter?

I start pondering where I stand in life, and nothing feels right. I have a doctorate in Humanities, but no job. I want to become a TV journalist, but my application is immediately rejected: as a foreigner, I am not allowed to be trained, let alone employed by the Swiss public broadcaster. Should I return to Germany, where I have better chances? I have always been homesick for this country, whose crimes I detest. But Volker refuses to go back. He has a job as an assistant at the University of Zurich and a chance to become a professor here. We have used up my money, and I am therefore dependent on my husband – a situation I had vowed to never get into. Although I find a low-paying job at a film production company in Zurich, I am frustrated. I enjoy producing films, but all we make is commercials. I don't learn to work as a journalist here. So in my mind things are going from bad to worse.

I run away with a colleague. It isn't a love story, we both know that, but we feel we are in the same situation: we just want to get away, and as far as possible! I want to travel to Cuba, to help the revolutionaries harvest sugar cane. But we only make it to the Dominican Republic, where P. and I separate. Happy and by now more self-confident, I continue my travels alone. In Puerto Rico, I have a job prospect and have just met an interesting man. But suddenly I am overcome by a massive homesickness for Volker. After three months in the Caribbean, I go back to him remorsefully. I can still see him standing by the entrance of the house he had moved to in the meantime with the commune – his arms stretched out to welcome me.

Searching for Fame and Fortune

I started my search for fame and fortune in San Diego, California. I first lived with my Aunt Ceil. Now, the Evans are not
what you would call a close-knit family. Aunt Ceil, my father's
sister, came to visit when we were living in Brewster twice, both
times with her boyfriend John. She was probably about forty
then and I thought she was style itself. She wore classy beige
wide leg pants and V-neck cashmere pullovers with some gold
chain dangling on her neck. She was very tall, thin and wore her
hair in a black bob. She lived in New York City and worked at an
advertising agency. The epitome of cool and in such contrast
to my own mother. Now don't get me wrong, now I think that
my mother's unique style was one of the most beautiful things
about her and made her stand out. She didn't care what people
thought of her. But white go-go boots, leopard skin mini skirts,
red cowboy hats and blonde hair waiting at the school bus stop
is not the kind of unique style that a twelve year old desires.
Needless to say, I pretty much idolized my Aunt Ceil.

When I was nineteen, Aunt Ceil had already moved from NY.
She and her boyfriend John split up and I think she was trying to get as far away from him as possible. So when I decided
that I wanted to become an actress, I thought that living with
Aunt Ceil in her apartment in San Diego would be great. I had
$2000 and the first thing I did was buy a 1954 Plymouth Plaza
for $200. I was sure my aunt would think it frivolous spending
and I decided not to tell her and parked it down the street. I got
a job at Jack LaLane's gym and attended Mesa College Drama
Department. I was on my way to becoming a star.

At the campus theatre, the Apolliad, I met M., who would become a lifelong friend and future roommate. There, I was cast

as an understudy in "The Shadow Box," a dancer in "Applause", a chorus part in "Baker Street", and my break-out-of-the-chorus role of Bette in "History of American Film."I learned how to build sets, use power tools and also took a film class. I have few regrets in life, but one is losing the first film I ever made. It starred M. and it was a 3min. existential silent film about a woman going insane behind the movie business. It was played to the song, "Welcome to the Machine," by Pink Floyd. When Professor Woodrow, "Woody", played the film, he paused and said, "Let's watch this again." Afterwards, he told me it reminded him of the films of Maya Deren. Now the really strange thing is that Deren and I seem to have more in common than just our film styles. Deren was born Maya Derenkowsky in Kiev, Russia April 29, 1917 into a Jewish family. My mother was born April 29, 1916. Deren died October 13, 1961. I was born October 13, 1960. Things come in threes, so the third connection/coincidence is that Deren attended Syracuse University where she studied journalism. My mother attended Syracuse University at the same time and majored in Art. My first desired career was journalism.

Before I was able to research Deren, we had to shoot our second film in class. I told the teacher that I wanted to film someone dancing without gravity, without a floor or a ceiling. He said the movie sounded quite like Norman McKlaren's 1968 "Pas de Deux." Years later I found out who else had made a similar movie, Maya Deren with her "A Study in Choreography for Camera" from 1945. Needless to say, I was hooked on film now and was determined to be a famous film actress and director.

I moved from my Aunt's apartment and after a short time at an apartment in Kearny Mesa, I moved to Ocean Beach to room with M.

It was she and I who moved up to Los Angeles together to try and make it in the Film Industry. We drove up in the daytime and looked at a few apartments. One was absolutely adorable.

A two bedroom Hollywood bungalow on Formosa Ave. between Sunset and Santa Monica Blvd. A beautiful light blue house with a small tiled fireplace. Bay windows, two bedrooms and a small backyard for six hundred dollars a month. We moved in two weeks later.

Fame and fortune were not as easy as sitting at Schwab's Drugstore in the Hollywood of the '80's. I really didn't know how to go about getting any parts. I auditioned in a "cattle call" for "Grease 2." Although I could dance, I wasn't as good as half of the hundreds of people that turned out for that audition. I tried getting an agent, but didn't have the

Larry Ann
in star pose

right pictures. I finally landed a job at the famous old restaurant, "The Cock and Bull" on Sunset Strip. I was a horrible waitress, but a great hostess and soon made friends with many of the producers and directors that would come in for lunch or during work or an after work drink.

There I found out that John Belushi died before anyone else knew and there I tried to chat up Timothy Dalton when he would sit near my hostess stand to eat. He never asked me out though, possibly because he was dating Vanessa Redgrave ... I would discuss what books I was reading with Alan Daviau, the cinematographer. In 1984, I told him I was reading "The Color Purple" and had just seen a great actress in San Francisco by the name of Whoopi Goldberg who would be great for the part ... Later when I saw Goldberg in the movie, I wondered if I had stayed in LA, would I have been able to somehow work on that film with Alan and Spielberg. I met many famous people at the Cock and Bull and if they were regulars, we were on first name basis. But I just couldn't break in to the film business. They saw me as hostess and then manager of the restaurant not as an actress. In the slow hours of the afternoon, I would show the producers and agents that frequented the restaurant bar headshots, composites, pictures of me that I was spending so much money on. They would look at them and say, "These are nice, Larry Ann. But, you need to get more pictures." Argh ...

So one day in 1984 I said that I didn't want to be an actress any more! I announced it to eight men at the bar. I said I wanted to be a script girl on a movie set and I got four offers right there. I didn't even really know what a script girl did, but dammit I wanted to work in movies and I'd sure as hell find out soon. I took the offer to be the personal assistant to Craig Rumar who was about to produce a film to be shot in Spain and away I went!

There I continued to work in the film industry with many companies, but mostly with Juan Piquer Simon a great director of Spanish B Series Horror and Adventure Films. I met my future husband there and really adopted Spain as my second homeland.

A Child

My son would agree straight away that I am a very curious person. He says that I, as a journalist, get people to tell me things that they don't really want to reveal. And he jokingly adds:

"And you do the same at home with your loved ones!"

Only, the tone of his voice indicates that he doesn't like it at all ... In fact, curiosity is probably the part of me that keeps me going inside. Maybe because I so early on in life was surrounded by people who had so many secrets? Because there was so much going on that I didn't understand?

Simon is born on May 30, 1975. The baby announces its arrival a few days early, just as Volker has travelled to a conference in Germany. My mother steps in and is with me during the birth. It is not the contractions that cause me the most pain, but my back. Here, in the delivery room, I feel as helpless as a beetle that has fallen on its back. But I still manage to worry if the situation is not too much for my mother, who sits there full of compassion.

The two events in life that make us dizzyingly blissful are falling in love and the birth of a child. Provided the child is wanted. Such a child can give us superhuman powers. And these powers are also what we need in order to cope with a life that changes completely. Simon is an easy baby – he laughs a lot, is infinitely curious too and therefore always on the move. The only time we don't have to keep a constant eye on him is when he sleeps. With my son, I catch up on everything that I missed out on as a child. I enjoy myself immensely when he smears the spinach from the plate onto the kitchen tiles, and even when he kicks about angrily in my arms. I try to make sure that he never has to experience fear, like I did when my mother left me alone in the house. Unfortunately, my son also struggles with anxieties when he is five years old. He wakes up from bad dreams and leaves me completely helpless.

Shortly before Simon's birth, I finally get offered a job at the Swiss national broadcaster. The following October I am already shooting my first short film and soon get the chance to make longer documentaries. In a film about genetic analysis I portray a girl suffering from an incurable metabolic disease. She confides in me how a twenty-year-old feels about knowing that she has at most ten years left to live. And then, in 1990, I am sent to Peru to make a film. "Hope is the Last Thing You Give Up," tells the story of six-year-old Elvis from Lima. He was picked up from the streets by an NGO that takes care of children. 'Terre des hommes' runs a children's home in Lima, and Elvis lives here, but he keeps on running away to live on the streets. Going home is not an option. His mother does not accept him – she even claims that he is not her child. As a newborn, he was first held back from her at the hospital, and she was told that he had died immediately after birth. But after two days, the baby was brought to her nonetheless. He was probably going to be sold, but the sale had failed, as the child had a slight clubfoot. Even though he was unmistakably similar to her, the mother did not want to accept the child any more.

Elvis and I have an instant liking for each other. For a moment I wonder whether we should adopt him. At the time, my own son is thirteen years old. How good his life is in comparison – even though I always feared that I was a bad mother. But he also has his father, a modern man, who looks after him – and not only during my absences. He inherits his sense of reality: like Volker, Simon is no friend of spontaneous decisions motivated by too much emotion. Together, they make it clear to me, that none of us three want to turn our lives completely upside down. And Elvis, who has learned to fight his way through the most adverse circumstances, entirely on his own, would definitely not be happy in Switzerland.

Larry Ann Has a Son

My son was born in Spain. My husband and I were living in a
new development called Tres Cantos outside of Madrid. I had
just finished working on a film, "Blood of a Poet." I was asked
to be the dialogue coach on the film, since they were having a
hard time finding one. I had worked at that time in many different positions on films, Production Secretary and Coordina-
tor, 1st and 2nd Assistant Director, Line Producer and Dialogue Coach, but I was 8 1/2 months pregnant and I really didn't
want to work on any film. But I accepted since they said they
were going to continue to look for a replacement while I was
working on the film. I had a great time, Giancarlo Giannini
was one of the actors in the film and was just brilliant. As I was
as big as a house, I was treated like a princess by all of the cast
and crew. I especially remember lunch times. I would go up
to the catering wagon and there the Spanish chef would tell
everyone to step aside because "Here comes mi niña. What do
you want to eat today mi niña? I will make you anything." I
never ate so well! We were filming in Granada, one of three or
four of the most beautiful places in the south of Spain. After
we wrapped in Granada, the film went on to other locations
and I went back to Tres Cantos.

Alex was born January 26, 1996. I call him Alex but his whole
name is a bit longer. Alexander Lorenzo Geronimo Calvo
Evans. Yes … Geronimo. I had picked out the name Alexander
because Alex is pronounced just about the same in English
and Spanish, but no one in my family really liked it. My father said they would call the boy, "Al" and he hated that name,
probably because he got on so terribly with his father, Albert.
I think my mother didn't like it because my father didn't like
it, so she would call me and give me other suggestions. One
time I got her on the phone and she was so excited. She said "I

know what you should name the boy!" and I said "What?" and she said, "Geronimo!" Well I started to laugh but then I realized she wasn't laughing. She was completely serious. Because of my mother's upbringing in Colorado I think she thought Geronimo, the great Apache medicine man and leader was an awesome name. But the name had gone through some transitions in American slang and since WWII was used to express exhilaration when jumping out of a plane ... I could just see how his life would be made into a veritable torture chamber in school with a name like Geronimo. So, because I loved my mother so much, I added it as a third name. His second name, Lorenzo, is a translation of Larry. Well, really Lawrence, there is no "Larry" in Spanish but close enough.

The Search with L.

It takes twenty years before I make another attempt to find Laramie Evans. My son is nineteen years old, he is about to finish high school and will soon leave home to study in Italy. I am hoping he doesn't notice how much I'm panicking about the imminent separation.

My mother died eleven years ago. She was only sixty-three years old. Alcohol destroyed her life, and we, her children, had to look on helplessly. We managed to persuade her three times to undergo rehabilitation, but all three times she suffered a relapse. She was a beautiful woman right to the very end. But her inside, her emotions, had been eroded by alcohol. The drinking probably came from a desire to feel nothing, to numb all feelings of guilt and her agonising fears. But it also destroyed her ability to rejoice and, above all, to love. She could be angry, even mean, with everyone and everything around her – even us children. And meanwhile, instead of pity I also started feeling anger towards her. Anger about the fact that she did not want to change. Anger about what she did to us. But maybe she rejected my advice and offers of help because she felt they were presumptuous – one can't reverse the role of mother and child just like that. At the very end, she lived a secluded life in Cologne, with only her dog, and did not let anyone come close to her.

My siblings both lived in Berlin. My brother had become a journalist, my sister a lawyer. We were very close. As long as we could remember, we had taken care of our mother and supported each other.

When my sister L. and I fly to New York, she has just broken up with her boyfriend. And I have just surfaced of a two year creative block. We want to blow away the cobwebs and travel to an exciting place together. We both choose New York. And, since we're so close, we might as well rent a car and drive to New Jersey. To the horse farm where Laramie Evans used to live, or – who knows – still lives.

I fool myself into thinking I'll be relaxed about it all. L. and I stay at the legendary Hotel Algonquin, which has been frequented by the New York intelligentsia since its opening – the perfect place for us ... All I have of Laramie Evans is an address from the year 1960, which played a role in the paternity suit and which I wrote to with my mother.

I am at the wheel of a rental car, and the closer we get to our destination, the more my heart and hands start trembling. Is the address correct? We did not receive an answer back in 1973. But what if we are suddenly about to stand face to face with Laramie? L., who has a good sense of reality, brings my feet back onto the ground:

"Now don't just think that he's sitting around the corner in a rocking chair!"

And indeed, things turn out to be not quite that simple. There is no longer a horse breeding farm at the address on New Bedford Road, Spring Lake – there is a supermarket. We drive around the neighbourhood for about an entire hour. And we end up at the supermarket again.

"But it must be here!"

I park the car, we go inside, wander around the shop a bit, before asking for the manager. Yes, it is quite possible that there once was a horse ranch here. But that must have been at least ten years ago. No, he did not work here then. Who could one ask? The friendly man takes us to his office and goes through numerous folders for us. We find out when the farm was sold and to whom, and when the supermarket was built. The man is also kind enough to make some phone calls for us. Finally, he mentions a veterinarian, who apparently worked at the ranch regularly. This man, too, is happy to help. It only takes one hour before we can meet him at the supermarket.

But my hopes are shattered again: the veterinarian does not remember a Laramie Evans. I show him a photograph – but even that does not jog his memory. I can't give him any other information, I don't even know what Laramie was doing on this farm.

How old might he be now? Is he still alive? I don't know the year he was born, but he has no doubt passed seventy. So time is running out, if I still want to meet him. But doubts start nagging me. Why did he never look for me? Even if he was very disappointed with my mother – why was he not interested in his daughter? What else happened that I don't know about?

Lyons Affects Larry

Lyons. Lyons of my youth was always a happy place for me. Well, Lyons was the end of the road for Larry and Ann and it turned out to be an unhappy place for all. My Uncle Howard had died in 1972 so my Aunt Doll and Nana were living in the house alone. In the beginning it was to be just another layover in Lyons, until either Daddy won the trial against his employers or until another job came through. At first it looked like there would be another job for Larry, but the new quarter horse track that was supposed to come to pass never did during those years and Larry found himself stuck, in Lyons. Ann was too far away from the bustle of the tracks and during these years was only commissioned to paint a few horses. I, again, had to make a whole new set of friends. I was again the new girl, to be looked at sideways, stared at, or laughed at while I tried to find the niche where I fit which was a lot easier in third grade, not so much in ninth.

The house was too small for the five of us. My aunt gave up her room and put a bed in the upstairs hall, outside of my mother's studio. My parents took her room. I moved into my mother's old room, a tiny room off of my parents bedroom and Nana's room was downstairs in the master bedroom off of the living room. We settled into a routine; I went to school down the street, my aunt went down in the cellar to groom the poodles, Nana stayed mainly in her room or if it was summer, out in the garden, my father sat in his chair and my mother sat in hers, with Little Bo Peep the poodle on her lap, waiting.

In 1975 Nana caught pneumonia and died in the hospital and then the fighting began in earnest. At five o'clock a silent bell would ring and drinks were served. A Vodka Martini for my mother, a whiskey ginger ale for my father, a scotch on the rocks for my aunt and the tv for me. Every night they would drink and every night my aunt and my father would start to argue. It ended with my parents retreating to their room upstairs and my aunt slamming the door to her room, now in the master bedroom. Luckily it was the late seventies and there were drugs, lots of them which I began experimenting with the summer after my grandmother died. Also lucky for me, I wasn't too stupid and researched everything I used and stayed away from the really addictive stuff like heroin. Most everything else was okay. Soon the generation gap widened enough so now I was arguing with my parents too. My father was so strict during those years. He wouldn't let me ride with anyone in a car, so I had to be dropped off down the street. I couldn't stay out as late as anyone else, so I had to learn how to sneak out after they went upstairs, which was usually right after dinner. After I graduated, I wanted to move to California, to be an actress, but didn't have enough money. I began working two jobs and relations broke down at my house so bad I ran away. I lived in the woods in a tent for a while, then with a friend and her mother. I'm not sure what prompted me to go back, but around November of 1979 I went back to the house, my parents and I made up and everybody gave me money. So along with the money I saved from my jobs, I had two thousand dollars. Enough to move to San Diego.

My mother later said the saddest thing to me. She said, "You hated this house so much, you moved as far away as you could and you never came back, except to visit." But what she didn't know was that I moved away to become rich and famous and to make enough money to finally move them out of that house. All of them. To set my father up with his own private golf course and my mother with a race track and my aunt with the apartment in the city that she always wanted and never got. I tried, I accomplished many of my dreams, but the rich part never materialized and the three of them stayed, in Hell.

It's Always on my Mind

At the film festival in Locarno I watch ‚Life is Beautiful' by Roberto Benigni. It's a glorious summer evening, and the film is shown in the open air on the Piazza Grande. I have gone to the screening on my own and manage to get a highly coveted seat in a restaurant on the square with a good view of the large screen. I have just eaten my favourite pizza, and I am excited to see the film. I know that it will not be light fare.

Benigni tells the story of a Jewish bookseller during Mussolini's fascist regime, who is deported together with his young son to a Nazi concentration camp. Benigni's father spent two years in the camp at Bergen-Belsen, and ‚Life is Beautiful' is partly based on his experiences. The great comedian himself plays the role of the father, who conceals the cruel realities of the camp from his son and make him believe that it is all just a game. The winner, he says, gets a toy tank as a prize.

In the last scene, the small boy stands on the large square of the concentration camp, lost. His father has just been shot, but he does not know that. But we in the audience have heard the shot. The other inmates have all been expelled from the camp, but even this the boy knows nothing about when he crawls out from the hiding place that his father showed him. The boy stands there all on his own and tries to understand. At this moment, a huge American tank drives onto the square. The hatch opens, and a GI leans out of the vehicle. He says with an infinitely friendly voice:

"Are you all alone here, kid?"

I have to cry – with a force that is only felt when something deep inside you has been touched.

Moving to Lyons, Yet Again

My husband, the two-year-old Alex and I moved back to Lyons in 1998. My parents needed me and I needed to be there for them. As I was growing up they gave me everything I needed. Like when I moved to California in 1979 I didn't make enough money to support myself and my parents would send me money sometimes. I didn't know it at the time, but they would sell their jewellery and some antiques in the house to get that money for me.

They never said they needed me to come home, they were always, "Fine, we're doing fine!" Every time I called, they were fine. I packed up the house in Spain and Alex and I came over first, my husband sold the large furniture and came a few months later.

My father had quit smoking in 1972 after his heart attack, but it wasn't soon enough. He was hooked up to an oxygen machine and my mother weighed about ninety-five pounds. My Aunt Doll couldn't see, but was still clipping a couple of poodles a week. There was a nurses aide that would come in and help around the house a couple of days a week and when I saw her, I thought, that should have been me. She sat in the living room in a small chair between my mother and father and she wrote checks out of my father's checkbook to pay their bills. I was jealous of the intimacy that she held with my parents. That should have been me.

Daddy no longer changed out of his pyjamas and robe. He said if Hugh Hefner could walk around in pyjamas all day long, why couldn't he. My mother never looked at him with any less love because of it. I had a smoking jacket made for him out of velvet with his initials on the pocket, he wore it sometimes but mostly he liked the softer one that I bought from the store for him.

Mommy loved Alex. I have a picture of him sitting on her lap, both wearing baby blue. Her arthritic fingers are trying to hold on to him, but they hardly did the job of fingers anymore. More like unbending pieces of wood, carved or shaped by someone who had never seen her graceful slender hands working a small tiny paintbrush creating the sheen of sweat on one of the horses she brought to life on canvas.

Daddy was different. I'm sure he must have loved Alex, I mean, it was his grandchild. But he could no longer see because of advanced macular degeneration of the eyes. He no longer moved very much because of the line that tied him to the oxygen machine. He would sit in his chair and point at Alex. "Larry Ann. Larry Ann! What is The Boy doing??" The boy, not Alex, but "The Boy." I capitalise it in my mind, like a name. As I said, Daddy never liked the name Alex, even though I promised him I wouldn't let anyone call him "Al". I have kept my promise.

I only remember him saying two things about Alex: "What is The Boy doing?" and "He has you wrapped around his little finger." Yes, Daddy, he does.

So the house in Lyons was too full again. Again two families blended to try and help each other. It didn't work out the first time, I was determined it would work this time.

We set up the two-year-old Alex in my old bedroom right outside my parents bedroom, my aunt slept in the 1st floor bedroom, and my husband and I slept in the small den off the living room while we renovated my mother's 2nd floor art studio into a bedroom. It must have been sad for her to see the room she had known as her space to create those beautiful paintings being turned into a bedroom. But, she was very happy to have us there. Poor Alex, it wasn't long before people started disappearing from the house.

My aunt was actually the first to go but the last to die. She went to go have an operation, they had found colon cancer. They told her to prep at home, eighty-two years old. She went to the hospital and when I went to go visit her before the operation, she was slurring her words. I asked the nurse what was wrong and she said "Oh, your aunt had a slight stroke in the night." We'll, I guess a "slight stroke" wasn't enough to postpone the procedure and they operated on her. She never came out of the hospital, she went straight to the nursing home where she stayed until she died in 2001.

In 1999 my mother got a flu shot and immediately got the flu. She got so sick she went to the hospital and there she became even worse. After five days she asked me to take her home and I did. The doctors advised against it, they said she wouldn't even make it home in the ambulance. She did. My father asked me why I brought her home. "Do you want her to die here?" he asked me. I told him that she asked me to bring her home and I did. She knew she was too weak, that nothing was going to make her better and she knew she didn't want to die in the cold sterile hospital room with nothing but nightmares around her. We set up my father's chair beside the bed that was placed in the den. There she lasted a day and a half before peacefully passing away on Jan. 6th, three kings day. I'm sure they helped her in her passage to the other side in which she believed so fiercely.

The house was more still without the loving presence of my mother. My father didn't move too much from his chair in the living room. His chair that faced her empty chair.

Life is Finite

Since my journey with L. to New Jersey, ten years have once again passed. Ten short years. I was diagnosed with breast cancer but got off lightly: I did not need a mastectomy and did not have to endure chemotherapy. But in 2002, a mammography once again reveals a lump in the chest. Within forty-eight hours, I am lying on the operating table. I am convinced that the cancer has flared up again. This time I am certain that I will not be able to avoid chemotherapy. Would I even be able to muster enough optimism to endure this agonising treatment? The days become oppressively long, until I finally get the result of the biopsy examination.

I am walking around my beloved old town of Zurich when my mobile phone rings. My gynaecologist tells me that the lump was a harmless calcification. I can hardly believe it and try to find somewhere to hold on to. Then, I run home to immediately share my incredible joy with everyone, laughing and crying. Volker embraces me. He, too, is infinitely relieved, and suggests that we celebrate by flying to Spain. Simon has just finished his master's degree in Political Science in Berlin and has hurried home to my side from his graduation party. He wants to join us, so all three of us head off together. As soon as we arrive in Malaga, we take our bikes to the beach. With my newfound carefreeness, I cycle along the beautiful, palm-lined beach promenade without holding onto the handlebars, my arms gliding through the air. We swim all day. In the evening, we go dancing in the open air, and Simon flirts with the most beautiful girl in the whole disco. At four o'clock in the morning, we finally all go to bed.

The next day, I have a painful abdominal infection. In all the euphoria I had forgotten that I had just had surgery and was no longer a young girl, but fifty-eight years old. I had gotten away, but I now realise clearly that I no longer have my whole life in front of me. It is not possible to postpone things that really matter to me.

Paul died five years ago, at the age of eighty. The years of mourning are over, and the loss will always hurt – but by some miracle, I have also become freer. Free from the feeling of betraying him if I seek out my biological father. Maybe many adopted children know this feeling. And I therefore decide to now do everything in my power to pursue one consistent goal: to find Laramie Evans.

In August 2004, I fly to California to the wedding of Christy, the daughter of my friend Linda. In the meantime, I have told Linda about the secret of my American father. And she immediately has an idea as to how we can look for him. Her sister-in-law Marje was a soldier in the US Army and has access to the archives. She is also an avid genealogist.

Linda and I embrace. The last time we saw each other, her daughter, who is now getting married, was four years old. Our friendship has survived the many years and the distance of an entire ocean unscathed. The wedding begins at a restaurant overlooking the bay of Laguna Beach, followed by a church wedding and a party. Linda's sister-in-law and I hit it off immediately.

It had taken me almost my whole adult life to find Laramie Evans. I had written a letter, searched out an address, contacted veterans organisations from World War II and lately also searched the internet. It takes Marje two weeks to find him in the army records: the man with the extraordinary first name and the commonplace surname. Laramie Evans. Officer of the

456th AAA Battalion, at first in Patton's Third, then in the Seventh Army. To begin with, I refuse to believe it. He has existed in my imagination for too long to be a human being of flesh and blood! Besides, not all the details seem right to me. From my mother I learned that Larry came from New York, and that he kept mentioning his beloved sister, who also lived there. Why would he have been born in Liverpool?

"Do You Believe in Heaven?"

One day I was looking in a drawer, you know that drawer, we all have them. Where everything is thrown. I doubt you have one like the one in Lyons. It is about two and a half feet long and people have been putting things in this drawer since 1939. You can find just about anything from batteries to dead people's reading glasses. So I think I was looking for a battery when my father asked, "Do you believe in Heaven?" Now daddy is what I call a social talker. In social situations, he's a great conversationalist, but at home I remember him as a quiet man. A thinker. He speaks when he is spoken to and usually doesn't come at you with theological questions. My mother once said that Daddy changed to the Catholic religion for her. Changed from what? I didn't ask, of course. So I looked at him and he waited. Is he asking me if people will be reunited with those they love in Heaven? Or is he just asking about the Heaven that priests talk about? I said that I have my own ideas on what happens after death. I said that we are made up of energy and that I didn't think that energy would stop just because our bodies died. I told him I thought that energy went on to take another form in another place, but that it wouldn't stop long there either. So I didn't come right out and say "No," but I didn't say "Yes," either. He looked at me and nodded. "Do you believe in God?" I told him that I didn't think that you could take all the components of this world and shake them up for a billion years and create this perfect yet fragile ecological balance that we have on this planet, so "Yes," I believe in a higher form, a greater intelligence that could be called "God." He nodded his head and went back to sit down in his chair. I suspect that he thought about what I said and what my mother, a very devout Catholic, believed and I imagine he thought on it for a long time. But he was a man of little words and he never spoke of it again, nor asked me another theological question. Up until that time the only theology that I had ever heard from my father was one sentence, "There are no atheists in fox holes." I asked him what that meant and he explained that while in the war with the bombings and gun fire, the men would dig long deep trenches, it must have seemed like a grave, really. Night sky lit up only with shots of gun fire, the smell of sweat and dirt all around, your feet cold and damp in the wet earth. He said that everyone would be praying to God to spare them and deliver them from this Hell. "There are no atheists in fox holes, Larry Ann." At the end of his life, Lyons was now his fox hole.

After my mother's death my father lasted only six months longer. I remember I was working for the radio station and doing a remote broadcast from the Wayne County Fair in August. I got the call that my father had been taken to the emergency room, but by the time I got there he was gone. Congestive heart failure. Although he quit smoking at about 54 it wasn't soon enough when you start smoking at nine.

I can only imagine what my son, this small little boy just three years old thought every time someone passed away. He was so young it must have seemed like they just disappeared into thin air from the house. So we stayed in Lyons to raise Alex in the house that held the furnishings and belongings of three generations of my family.

The house in Lyons is a reoccurring place throughout my life. A happy home for me in my childhood, an unhappy home for my parents and I when I was going to high school. As an adult my own marriage didn't work out there, but, for Alex I hope it was and remains a happy place to live.

I Find Larry Ann

Marje and I are now looking for Laramie Evans on the internet. But what we find comes as a blow: it is his obituary. The man I consider to be my father died five years ago in Lyons in upstate New York. The voice of reason tells me that this was to be expected after so many years – but I am saddened and disappointed.

But wait – the obituary mentions Laramie Evans's two children. I know about his son Barry, who was born one year after me, from one of the letters that Larry had written to my mother. But a daughter? I had no idea about her. Should I write to them? Would I dare? What, if I once again get no answer? Could I handle it? And who should I write to – him or her? I finally muster all my courage, and the pendulum swings in favour of the woman. Luckily, as it turns out.

I write a letter to Larry Ann Evans. I attach two pictures, one of myself and one of the man from my mother's photo album. My hands tremble a bit when I deliver the letter at the post office. It's Thursday.

A Letter from Overseas

The mail came just like any other day. I pulled out the one that looked a little extra long, and I got really excited. Extra long meant A4 Paper from overseas. Maybe Juan Piquer who I had worked with for so long was writing me from Spain. I took the letter into the den. No matter what time of day, it's always dusk in the den. It's dark and there with the bear, the bobcat, the badger and the deer's head with his one eye now drooping and ready to drop any day, I opened the letter with excitement. A photo slid out onto the floor of the den. I bent to pick it up and there, with the afternoon light shining lazily through the dust-covered panes of the den windows, lay a picture of my father. But he was wearing an expression I had never seen. This father that I have always known, was at that time in this picture on the floor someone I didn't know. Years earlier I had found a 16 mm film of my mother. She was with her first husband and people I didn't know or had never even heard about. On the film, her movements and expressions seemed to be of an Ann Collins that I didn't know. We all seem to change for different persons.

The "daddy" in the photo on the floor was looking daringly into the camera. He was a wolf, I mean this photo just blew my mind. He had his army uniform on and looked pretty much like a male model. I stooped to pick up this photo of my father that I had never seen and then proceeded to read the first sentence of the letter that came with the photo.

"If this is your father, then I am your sister."

The Reply

Three days later, the email arrives, and its subject line jumps out from all the other emails:

Subject: Laramie Evans = Dad

For a moment, my world comes to a standstill.

I open the email, and read:

Dear Marion, WOW! Yes, that's my father in the picture. And looking at your picture, you have his eyes. (...)

It's a long, beautiful email. I read it again and again, word by word. Larry Ann Evans did not only respond immediately. She is happy that I exist! It takes an entire day before I am capable of writing back to her.

Dear Marion,

WOW! Yes, that's my father in the picture. And looking at your picture, you have his eyes. I knew that he had a daughter in Germany, but never knew your name or where you lived. I know that my father's first wife, whom he had a son with   did not want to wait for him through the war years, and wrote him goodbye while he was overseas. I would love to hear the story of how my father met your mother and who she was and as much as you can tell me! My father was wonderful, but didn't talk much about his war years. This is not the first surprise I've had since his death. He also forgot to tell me that both of his parents were Jewish. I found out from my cousin (Perry Evans daughter) I hope you're not in shock now!

I can't believe you're a filmmaker!!! I lived in Spain for 13 years working in films! My husband, Ignacio, is Spanish and we have one son, Alexander, who is 9. You don't look old enough to have a son that is 30!

I see your picture is taken in California. Larry had a sister that lives in San Diego. She was doing well until just a few months ago when she had a stroke and is now in a nursing home, her name is Cecelia and she is about 84. There are two other siblings, Perry (91 this year and lives in Long Island), and Millie (a few years younger and lives in Florida).

Thank you so much for getting in touch. Write back soon. Ignacio and I might be taking a trip to Spain in the summer of 2006, I would love to meet up with you somewhere in Europe. We have lot's of time to plan it.

I have attached some pictures to this email, I'll send you more later. I'll get some of my/our father scanned and send you some of those too.

A big hug,

Larry Ann

Larry Ann's very first
email to me

(...) I knew that he had a daughter in Germany, but never knew your name or where you lived. I know that my father's first wife, whom he had a son with (B.) did not want to wait for him through the war years, and wrote him goodbye while he was overseas. I would love to hear the story about how my father met your mother and who she was and as much as you can tell me! My father was wonderful, but didn't talk much about the war years.

This is not the first surprise I've had since his death. He also forgot to tell me that both of his parents were jewish. I found out from a cous-in (Perry Evans' daughter). I hope you're not in shock now!

I can't believe you're a filmmaker!! I lived in Spain for 13 years and working in films! My husband, C., is Spanish and we have one son, Alexander, who is 9. You don't look old enough to have a son that is 30!

(...)

A big hug,

Larry Ann

When I open the attachment with the photographs she has sent, I once again have to catch my breath. It's as if I am looking at a picture of myself from a decade ago. Larry Ann is thirteen years younger than me.

Marion Comes to Lyons

A sister! I have a sister! Wow! And I think that is the first word that I wrote in the letter back to Marion. We continue to converse and find out how many similarities we have. We both have distinctive laughs, we both work in the Film Industry and we even both started out as script girls! She lives in Switzerland, but also has a house in Malaga. Malaga! When I went to Spain I lived in Puerto Banus first, about 40 miles from Malaga. She has one son, Simon. I have one son, Alex. I look at her picture. She looks so much like Daddy and she got the height too, I'm only 5'6", she's 5'8" . We look so much alike, it's amazing. We are planning to meet, she is coming to Lyons!

A sister ...

My husband went to pick up Marion at the airport because Alex had a Christmas concert he was performing in. I was so excited I could hardly concentrate on my son's performance, nor my surroundings. When she walked into the theatre, I couldn't believe the similarities, we looked more like twins, even with the age difference. I felt like running toward her, it felt like I had known her all my life, we threw our arms around each other and hugged like long lost friends.

A sister ... My sis.

The First Visit

Rochester has had some heavy snowfall, and I arrive late. There had been an abrupt onset of winter, and my flight from New York was initially cancelled. Then, after waiting anxiously for two hours, we have been given the go-ahead to take off. By now, I have been travelling for 14 hours, but as far as I'm concerned it might as well have been days – even then, I would not be able to close an eye out of sheer excitement. In New York, as always, there were endless queues in front of the passport controls. One is not exactly welcomed with open arms to this country – do Americans who travel to Europe also have to answer questions such as whether they are gay or if they have taken drugs at some point in their lives? Today, I don't care about any of this. I am being cheerfully expected by the woman, whose existence I have only known about for two months. My sister.

I have been thinking for a long time how I can drive away my impatience and make time pass on the flight, and the book I have brought with me manages to captivate me for a while. And yet, my thoughts keep wandering, to Larry Ann. It took me 32 years to find her, and it wasn't even her I'd been looking for, but my father.

Today, as I am travelling to meet her, I already know a lot about her. We were both amazed at how similar we are. When Larry Ann wrote "Are you also known for your laugh?", I had to laugh out loud – after all: I even go as far as claiming that I met my husband thanks to one of my fits of laughter.

And now, the first meeting with my sister. We have already talked once on the phone. Hearing each other's voices was another major step. As a result, there were also a few shy pauses in the conversation. But I really liked her voice and her manner.

She has planned this evening down to the last detail, which I find reassuring.

The high school auditorium is packed with parents, grandparents, siblings and friends of the young musical performers, and the show is in full swing when I enter the room. Larry Ann catches sight of me immediately, and she makes her way through the crowded row of seats towards me – and the two sisters who have never met embrace before even taking a proper look at each other. She looks like she's thirty, even though she is in her late forties. In her fashionably tailored brown suit made of fine, soft fabric, she looks slender, almost a bit fragile – but this might also be due to the slight bashfulness that overcomes us both. I have no idea any more what the high school was performing – I don't even think I registered any of it. It means the world to me that I am sitting here next to my sister and that Larry Ann's son Alexander has now come onto the stage. His eyes almost pop out when he sees me in the auditorium and he almost forgets about his role.

That night, the two of us and Larry Ann's husband sit together a long time enjoying red wine and Jamón Serrano. In Europe, it is now six o'clock in the morning ... And the next day, it all continues: Larry Ann and I tell each other our lives, ask each other questions, wallow in documents. Soon, the table is strewn with mountains of paper. There is no doubt any more that her father was also my father, we do not need a DNA test to confirm this. We forget about everything around us. Had her husband not cooked a meal for us at some point, we would have happily starved.

Larry Ann knew I existed because her parents mentioned me on a couple of occasions. Her father, she recalls, once talked about signing a paper. A document, where he testified that he wasn't my father. She remembers that this was somehow for my own good. I freeze. My mother asked Laramie Evans for a signature! The document was probably meant to increase the likelihood of winning the paternity suit, or at least to reach a settlement. But it is hard to imagine that a court would have taken any such testimony seriously. I will never know precisely, as my mother destroyed all documents.

I am touched by how spontaneously my sister is willing to share her father with me. I don't just mean his memory, but the paternity. We now just call Larry "our father". She tells me what kind of a person he was, and she talks about our grandparents, who died when she was very young. I end up crying twice that week: when I hold one of Larry's ties in my hands, and when I see him in a video of Larry Ann's wedding. I knew the pictures of him, but moving images convey a much stronger feeling of meeting someone in person. I see his tall, slender figure, his gait, his serious face, a smile. He is wearing a striking red suit. Does he also speak in the video, did I hear his voice? I don't remember! Yet a person's voice is so important to me. But when one is overcome with great emotions, it is difficult to absorb several things at once.

| **Marion in Lyons**

It was so exciting bringing Marion home. There were so many things I wanted to tell her and show her. The first night that we were together is a jumble of images in my mind. She looked at the paintings on the walls and the beautiful portrait of my mother. Then, looking at the small portrait my mother painted of daddy she said, "This is our father!?" Our father ... Yes, that's our father!

I can't hardly begin to explain what it felt like for an only child to hear those words. I feel like even if he were alive, I would have been overjoyed to share him with her. Which is so strange, because as I have written, I was not very willing to share him with anyone. Not with the nurse's aide that was helping him, not with the photographer from so long ago who took our picture, not with anyone. But I felt that here was a person that I could share him with. I wouldn't be jealous of Marion if she had been able to have a relationship with Daddy. I'm sure he would have loved her. But she got there too late, he was already gone. It was probably a good thing because at the end of his life he had retreated so very far inside of himself, he hardly was the same man. He couldn't stand the oxygen machine, the line that tied him to it. He couldn't stand that he couldn't see to read. He couldn't stand the house, nor the small town of Lyons whose inhabitants look at even 2nd generation residents as outsiders and he couldn't stand the snow of upstate NY. Yes, it's better this way. I can tell her all of the wonderful things that I remember of my father, our father.

How well he played golf. What a snazzy dresser he was and his socks, red, the only color sock he owned. His jet black hair, which he insisted was chocolate brown in his youth. His long stride when walking. I showed her pictures of him kneeling beside a foal he just helped a mare birth and pictures of him when he was young and playing baseball in the streets of Brooklyn. I played my wedding video, just so she could see him move. When she sat down in the living room, I told her that was his chair. She had picked his chair to sit in. That's where he sat. I showed her the man that I wanted her to know and that I wanted to remember. Not the shuffling feet, but the long stride. Not the pajamas, but the polos. And not the depression, but the man, smiling, waving at the camera.

A Happy Outcome

I often wished I was someone else. Above all, somebody much, much braver. Why did I not steal mopeds as a teenager, to show the world how desperate and angry I was? Why did I not travel the world as an actress with a travelling theatre company, like I dreamed of for years? This other person would also have stubbornly looked for her father, and she would not have given up after the first hurdle. She would have found him while he was still alive.

But I was full of guilt and fear. Guilt towards Paul. Fear, that Laramie Evans might not be happy to see me. I am sure that would have destroyed me.

And therefore, I conclude that fate meant well for me. Instead of my father, I have found a wonderful sister. In Larry Ann's words: "It's as if we had always known each other." And we are far from the end of our journey. There is a new continent for us to discover – together.

We meet at least once a year. On her last visit, Larry Ann gave me Hemingway's novel "For Whom the Bell Tolls". She said it was our father's favourite book –he had read it over and over: the story of a great love during a war. The American soldier and the Spanish girl only have three days to live their love, then they are torn apart. Three days for an experience that can fulfil a lifetime.

The Red Socks

I don't know why I remember some stories so well and others I forget almost right after I hear them, but this is one of the ones that sticks.

Marion, her husband Volker and I are sitting around the long dining table in her house in Cortona, Italy. The fire is crackling in the immense chimney behind me and we have the best after-dinner conversations. This is where I tell her the red socks story.

"Red socks. No, not Red Sox the baseball team, but Daddy's red socks. He had many pairs of socks as most people do, but his socks were all red. I never thought anything of the red socks, but I must have asked him at one time because that's how I know the story of the red socks," I say.

"In WWII, Daddy got some sort of fungus on his feet from walking through the muddy ground, from standing in the damp trenches, from probably not having more than one or two pairs of socks, from probably all of this combined. He went to the platoon medic who I imagine prescribed some sort of salve. It didn't work. The crud got worse. So bad in fact, that Daddy said the medic told him if it didn't stop they would have to take his feet. Losing your foot or feet in the war because of a mine is one thing, but losing them to some creeping crud? It wasn't the medic, but another soldier that told daddy to start wearing red socks. His theory was that bugs, bacteria, fungus, whatever didn't grow as well in the color red. Daddy somehow got a hold of some red socks and started wearing them daily. The crud started receding. His feet began to heal and he never owned or wore another color sock again. Ever."

This story somehow sums up one part of our father's personality. His conviction that once something is decided upon, he will never change his mind.

Family

"We knew nothing about you," my uncle Percy says. He is a charming old gentleman aged 91 when Larry Ann and I visit him on Long Island. Our father's older brother insists on sending a limousine to collect us from the airport. He survived Larry. What good fortune for me! Just like Larry Ann, he and his daughter Martha – our cousin – welcome me with open arms.

"And what if you had known back then that Larry had a daughter in Germany?" I ask.

"Oh, my wife Adelaide and I would not have liked that at all."

"And today you like it?"

"Yes, of course. Times have changed!"

Martha is a few years older than me and takes care of her old father, just like she took care of her mother before she passed away. The father and daughter live in a small, typically American suburban house.

During this visit, I learn many new details about my father. The two brothers lived very different lives. Both were born into a poor family. Percy was considered a bookworm, Larry was more the sportsman. Both of them worked at the age of fourteen to help support the family. Larry caught up with his high school graduation through evening classes. The life of his brother had one aim: security. He married, had two daughters, regularly brought home money and bought a house. Larry, on the other hand, was a nomad. He married three times and had various jobs – from semi professional baseball player in his youth to businessman, to journalist and horse breeder. Just like his parents – who moved from one apartment to the next, because they could not pay the rent, and from one town to the next, constantly in search of work

– Larry went where opportunity would take him. He could adapt to any situation. There were high times, when money was in abundance, and low moments. Larry Ann and I both turned out like our father, even if my life seems more stable when seen from the outside.

Half a year later, we visit Millie, my father's sister, who lives in Florida. The eighty-six-year-old opens the door and first embraces Larry Ann, and then also me, as if it was the most natural thing in the world. Her blonde hair is prettily combed, she is meticulously made up, wearing sporty white trousers and a smart striped pullover – in other words: she looks at least 10 years younger than her true age. The table is lovingly and abundantly laid, and we are served bread rolls, various salads, cakes and pastries. As Millie tells us, she still plays golf. Only reading has become difficult for her, and she now needs a computer that greatly enlarges the type.

I think of my mother, who was born the same year as Millie, in 1920. This lady, my aunt, has an entirely different disposition. Like all Evans siblings, she had a difficult childhood and youth. When her father Albert, once again without a job, moved to Florida with her mother, she stayed behind in New York to take care for her twelve-year-old sister, and without any money. Relatives helped out here and there. Still a young girl, the pretty Millie then found her great love. She started a business with her husband and they were successful. And she now radiates joy and energy, and she is curious to know more about this niece who has so unexpectedly fallen into her house. I feel comfortable around her and hope to grow old like she did.

The Famous Radacekeeper

Marion and I are researching our daddy's family. We have been able to go back as far as the Patriarch of the family, Great Grandfather Abraham Evansky and his wife Rebecca who moved to the United States in 1903. On the 1910 census we see that their address was Brooklyn Ward 26, Kings NY and that their profession was Radacekeeper. Radacekeeper? What in the hell is a Radacekeeper we wondered. "Don't you know?" Marion asked. No, I had no idea what that profession was. We started to research the word. It didn't exist on Google, the search-god of all current knowledge. Impossible! Marion found a similar word when she started to search in Russian and Czechoslovakian that meant "whore" so we had a good laugh over that one. Not being satisfied that the word was sim-ilar enough to Radacekeeper we kept looking. I found that in professions from the 1800's a "keeper" was an attendant, a guard, a warden, or gamekeeper.

But still we found nothing about "Radace." We tried every-thing, Russian translator, Czech translator, Old English professions. Even Yiddish! Nothing. It was infuriating! Two and a half hours later we were just about to give up when I began to remember a story my father told me. One of his relatives was rich. He wouldn't give Daddy, nor his father, Albert, a job. He owned a shop in the Garment District of Manhattan. He was a tailor. As I thought more on the story, it seemed that our father was speaking of his grandfather ... What if Radacekeep-er was what the word sounded like from someone with an accent? Or maybe he was reiterating and saying the word in his native tongue! So we quickly looked up tailor Russian ... "Rezccik!" But it means "cutting machine." Next in Czech ... "Rezacka" Yes! Sounds like Radace! Again, sounds a bit like Radace and "keeper" could possibly sound like tailor. Maybe he was saying his profession in the both languages! Therefore, "Radacekeeper" turns into Rezcchik, Tailor. We think so. Sides, we're tired, we're hungry and we're going to eat.

The hysterics of the following night were uncontrollable!

"Radacekeeper!"

Whahahhhahhahhahha! Fits of laughter.

"Radacekeeper!"

Whahahhhahhahhahha! More fits of laughter.

The hysterics were born out of our research that night ... Marion and I finally broke down and spent the money for an ancestry research website since we kept knocking up against that locked door in our research.

We started a family tree and added Laramie Evans. Then changed it to George Evans and voila! Up pops the record of he, his brother, mother and father on the boat to the United States from Liverpool. But wait, their names are crossed off. Did they miss the boat? Could they not all of a sudden pay for the boat? We know they came back in 1916 so we kept searching and finally found another boat that they were listed on. We didn't find out any new details about them on that passenger list. We then tried "Rachel Newman" No records. "Rae Newman"? No records. Rae Neuman? Or is Rae derived from Rebecca? These name changes are infuriating ... Pretty much a dead end on the paternal grandmother. We went back to our father's father and typed in his father, Albert Evansky. After looking through quite a few of the hits we came upon the 1910 census and there they all were. Abraham, his wife Rebecca and all of the children born at that time. Albert, our grandfather and the oldest, then Samuel, Isidor, Dora and Dobe. Abraham was born in Odessa and spoke English and Yiddish. Rebecca spoke no English, just Yiddish and couldn't read nor write. We went back up to Abraham. He could read and write. We drew out finger across the line of age, address, profession ... Profession! RADACEKEEPER! ARGH! That archaic word again! But wait... the original census is actually handwritten! Looking closer it said, Radace dealer, yes, definitely dealer! Looking more at the bane of our current dilemma it doesn't say Radace it says PRODUCE! Produce dealer. He had a grocery store, or a cart ... With probably some radishes, we joked. So the census worker comes to the door, Rebecca 45 at that time, answers, probably cooking some cabbage or possibly radishes. She speaks no English and then after probably excruciating moments trying to decipher what she is talking about, the poor census bureau man goes away, scribbling Produce keeper in his worst handwriting ... Radacekeeper.

Mulberry Street
NYC 1900

Where Grandfather Grew up

I have become preoccupied with my father's parents. Under what circumstances did they leave Europe? I can't let go of the question as to why they were silent about their origins their entire lives – why the place they grew up in was just one big empty void for their children and grandchildren. What did they experience that made them want to banish it completely from their memories?

Certificate of
Naturalization, 1912

I admire the courage with which they set off towards new, un-known shores: to the United States, to freedom.

Were my grandparents witnesses, perhaps even victims of the pogroms that had been raging in the Russian Empire since the murder of Czar Alexander – when, once again, Jews became the scapegoats? I have read everything I could find about the time after 1861. I was most touched by the Odessa stories by Isaak Babel. Odessa – this much Larry Ann and I know – is where our grandfather Albert was born. In 1905, he arrived at Ellis Island as a twenty-three-year-old. We have found his naturalization document. One can clearly see that the "ky" has been scratched away from Evansky.

In "The Story of my Dovecot", Babel tells the story of the atrocious pogrom of 1904 in Odessa. The young Isaak is nine years old at the time and has just returned from the market, where his deepest wish has been fulfilled: three pigeons for his dovecot.

"Our house was empty. Its white door stood open, the grass by the dovecote was trampled down. Kuzma, our janitor, was the only one who had not left our courtyard. He was sitting in the shed next to my grandfather Shoyil's dead body, dressing him.

'The wind brings you in like a bad splinter' the old man said when he saw me. 'You were gone for ages … See how the towns-folk have hacked our grandfather down …'

Kuzma began sniffling, turned away, and pulled a perch out of the fly of Grandpa's trousers. Two perches had been shoved into Grandpa – one into his fly, the other into his mouth – and although Grandpa was dead, one of the perches was still alive and quivering."

Last year I travelled to Odessa and did some local research in the state archives. The historical documents have partly disappeared. Some of them have not yet been digitised, which meant that I had to read through hand-written documents. I do not speak Russian, and I therefore had somebody write the name Evansky down for me in Cyrillic letters: **ЕВАНСКИ**. I actually found a Baruch Evansky, who was registered with his family in the Moldavanka neighbourhood in 1904. Now a rundown, notorious area, Moldavanka used to be the city's Jewish neighbourhood, where also Babel's stories take place. I drove there and found the address. Instead of the house where my grandfather might have lived, there now lies a hospital. What happened to the inhabitants who did not flee from the barbarism?

5 | Larry Ann & Marion
Lyons, New York – 2005

Our Grandparents had a Hard Life

Our Grandparents, Albert and Rae Evans moved to Liverpool sometime around 1912/1913 and our father "George Irving Evans" was born there. There are a couple of stories in the family about why they left the States again and of course our father's side of the story doesn't line up very well with the other stories. His side is that his parents went overseas for a vacation, maybe their honeymoon and they got stuck there because WWI broke out. That's why he was born in England. Cousin Amee and her sister Martha had heard that Albert couldn't find a job in NY and when he did find one, he couldn't keep it. Rae had relatives in Liverpool, a store of some sort. They said it was a vegetarian store. So Albert and Rae went over to work in the store. At that time the Jewish Community in Liverpool was 11,000 strong. Anyway, the story goes on that a fight broke out between Albert and his family member in Liverpool because Albert was selling meat secretly from the store and he lost that job too.

Were there any vegetarian stores at that time? This is probably another story distorted by biased relatives remembering long ago events. Or like the theatrical game, "Telephone", when it's funny to see how a story can change by whispering it from ear to ear down a line of just 20 people. How a story must change through three generations of family. Maybe Rae's relatives were running a kosher butchery and Albert was selling unkosher meat!

In any case, it was back to the States with the two little boys, Percy and George, in 1916. Albert losing a job is a recurring theme. We hear from our Uncle that his mother, Rae had depression and the family was extremely poor. While our father always said he loved his mother very much, I don't think he liked his father at all.

When he spoke of his mother, I never got the feeling she was in a depressed state. Once he told me that when he would go home and visit her, after moving around with the minor league ball teams, she could not see very well. She wore these very thick glasses and she would ask him to pull out her grey hairs. One year he came home and she said, "pull out the black ones, leave the grey hairs!" He had told me she wasn't a very healthy woman, but he never said she lay around in bed, depressed as Uncle Percy remembered. We each remember those parts of our loved ones that we want, and obviously Daddy only wanted to remember the good ones. Maybe that's why there were so few stories of his parents, there weren't very many good times.

The Story of Us

It doesn't matter where we are, in a subway in New York, in a cafe in Cortona or in a trolley in Toronto, people are drawn to ask us if we are sisters. It's strange really, if you see two women that look alike sitting next to you on a bus or standing next to you on the street, usually you are not drawn to ask them if they are related. But it is different with us. We are quite animated and of course there is that thing about our laughter, it is very loud and freely escapes our lips. We look amazingly alike, and we have good genes, so we both look younger than our years, but one is thirteen years older than the other. Then there are the accents, one of us has a German accent, and the other an American one. So we understand when we are asked "Are you sisters?" their curiosity is greater than their fear of intrusion. When we answer yes, of course we must explain and begin to tell our story.

We're not sure when, but we got asked the question so many times, and we told the story so many times that we decided to write it down. Now both being from the film world,

you would have thought that we would have made a film, or documentary. But we have decided that this should be the first form that our story will take.

Marion and Larry Ann

THANKS

A very special thank to you, Marje. You have found Larry Ann. Without your engagement and great help, we would never have met.

We also thank: The Many bars and restaurants where we sat for hours revising our manuscript.

Annika Hartmann, editor for Bastei Lübbe

Volker and Simon Bornschier and Silja Haeusermann for all of their support

Alexander Calvo Evans for all of his support

Stuart Smart, and Kate Ennis who proofread the manuscript

Picture Credits

S: 15   Rheinisches Bildarchiv Köln, Claasen, Hermann,
         rba_d029228

S: 18   Wikimedia Commons. The heirs of the creator grant
         anyone the right to use this work for any purpose,
         without any conditions.

S: 20   Private photo

S: 26   F.A.Z. -Repro/Wolfgang Elmes

S: 30   Wikimedia Commons

S: 36   Private photo

S: 45   Private photo

S: 47   Private photo

S: 58   Private photo

S: 63   Private photo

S: 69   Private photo

S: 74   Private photo

S: 81   The U.S. National Archives | Public Domain

S: 85   Private photo

S: 90   Private photo

S: 114   Private photo

S: 128   Wikimedia Commons

S: 129   Private photo

S: 134   Private photo

CPSIA information can be obtained
at www.ICGtesting.com
Printed in the USA
LVHW031505090121
675852LV00006B/733